Cultivating Respect and Cooperation
in the Classroom and at Home

A Step-by-Step Guide for Teachers and Parents

3rd Grade - 12th Grade

Laurie Hunter

Published by Laurie Hunter
Austin

Cataloging-in-Publication Data
Hunter, Laurie
Cultivating Respect and Cooperation in the Classroom and at Home
A Step-by-Step Guide for Teachers and Parents, 3rd Grade – 12th Grade
1. Parenting. 2. Teaching. 3. Family & relationships. 4. Child rearing.
I. Laurie Hunter. II. Cultivating Respect and Cooperation in the Classroom and at Home
ISBN 978-0-9974882-0-3
LB 3011-3095   649.64 HU   2016906426

Printed in the U.S.
Published by Laurie Hunter
Cover design by *Pixelstudio*

Table of Contents

ACKNOWLEDGMENTS

I'd like to thank my three children and all the students I've had the honor of teaching over the years. You have made this book possible. Together, we will help other students overcome hurdles and achieve success. I want to thank my 6th grade summer school students. We learned from each other. Thanks also to my 8th grade students. You will always be my "newchildren." My deepest gratitude goes to the students of all ages and abilities I've privately worked with over these years. You are my heroes, each and every one of you.

For years, I have also had the honor of working with many parents and teachers. Thank you: Cathy Humphrey, Dawn Piper, Leela Fireside, Carol Gonsalves, Meenakshi Gautam, Laura Pittman, Lori Webster, Pam White, Stacy Swanick, Mona Knutsen, Madeline Mansen, Barbara Gottlieb, and Rebecca Albe. I wish I could name every one. Our experiences have contributed to different parts of this book. And because of you, we will help other parents and teachers cultivate respect and cooperation, and also hope, vision, teamwork, and small miracles.

Thank you: Juli Naranjo, Rebecca Everett, Marilyn Wooldridge, Mrs. Martin, Mrs. Desha, and all the devoted teachers, tutors, coaches, counselors, and parents that never give up on a child. Thank you for working with students who experience academic, behavioral, and social challenges. Your relevant, interactive, and meaningful instruction has helped students build skills and bring out the best in ALL your students.

Thank you to the school administrators who provide dynamic leadership to students of all abilities. Karon Rilling, Candace Hughs, April Glenn, and Brenda Cox, thanks for contributing to your schools and to my development and understanding.

Thanks to my parents and to my husband, Jeff, for your support. Most of all, thank you, God, for blessing my life with my parents, husband, three children, my students, their families, and all our challenges. Thank you for nudging me to write down our experiences so that we may share them and bring solutions and happiness to others.

HOW TO USE THIS BOOK

This book has the same qualities as an instruction manual, handbook, workbook, and journal. It is a systematic and explicit program structured in 21 steps for parents*, teachers, tutors, coaches, counselors, mentors, and school administrators who want to improve their child or students' behaviors in the classroom, at home, or in other learning environments.

Each step:

- Begins with an objective and compelling logic,
- Contains a lesson the reader can complete with a child or student(s), and
- Ends with an opportunity for the instructor or parent to journal.

Current books and programs contain an overwhelming amount of content. The content of this manual is based on my background, experience, and successes as a parent, teacher, and an advocate for children of all abilities. I understand the time constraints and emotional needs of struggling students, parents, and teachers. Therefore, I have chosen the most essential information, strategies, and techniques that have the most significant impact on children.

How to use this book for optimal results:

- Read through each step completely before working on it with a child or classroom of students.
- Work on the steps in the order they are presented in this book. Each step builds upon the previous steps. For example, if you have completed Steps 1 through 9, then you will have the cumulative knowledge needed to accomplish Step 10, which is to address patterns of inappropriate behavior. However, you may read Step 21 at any point.
- Complete the lesson with your child or student in each step to activate and improve their mindset. Each lesson contains actual wording you can read to them. However, study each one in advance, so it will come across smoothly and intelligibly. Older children can read the lessons with you.
- Complete one journal for each step. Scientific evidence supports that journaling is a powerful tool used to achieve success in resolving disagreements, understanding points of view, and reaching resolution to conflicts. Journaling helps us rehearse for

a future event. It can help us practice and prepare for what we want to say and do. It can unlock solutions to seemingly unsolvable problems.

Keep in mind, gaining respect and cooperation is a process, not a switch that you can simply flip on. It will take time, patience, experimentation, and practice. It is my goal to provide you with tools, strategies, techniques, wording, perspectives, and activities that will help you gain respect and cooperation. In turn, your child(ren) will become more successful, so your home, school, and other learning environments will become more positive places to develop skills and thrive.

Also, you may wonder why I did not make two separate books, one for parents and one for teachers. I did this intentionally, because I believe every reader will gain exponentially from receiving both perspectives. You may think some steps, such as Step 19, do not pertain to you, but every step will reveal how it is relevant to us all. So, please don't skip over any information. The constructive insight you gain from studying each step will increase your awareness and contribute to your child or students' respect and cooperation.

*Throughout the course of this book, I use the word parent to refer to any caregiver who may be a mother, father, stepparent, grandmother, uncle, foster parent, etc.

INTRODUCTION

Every day, teachers and parents face significant challenges in our modern classrooms and homes: disrespect, resistance, hostility, and lack of cooperation. Children are committing suicide and school shootings. We wonder why and who is to blame? We hear comments such as: school systems are ineffective, teachers are inept, parents are spoiling their children, classrooms are filled with students who come from broken homes, poverty, and multiple learning disabilities… What can we do? How can we connect with our children and teens in a way that increases their awareness, so that we can address these and other serious behaviors and issues?

Parents, teachers, tutors, counselors, and coaches can study the 21 steps in this book to stimulate awareness that can help our children and teens self-monitor and manage their behaviors. Step by step, in a cumulative fashion, we can help children improve their executive functions and increase their motivation. As we progress through the 21 steps, we can re-pattern our children's thoughts, words, and actions, so that we may cultivate respect and cooperation in the classroom and at home.

OUR STORY

First grade was dreadful for my twin sons, Preston and Warren. They would cry every day, begging to stay home from school. By the end of the school year their teachers and principal insisted that they repeat 1st grade because "they needed more time to mature." I didn't know then that they had dyslexia. But, I did know that another year of the same instruction was not the answer. I pleaded with the school to allow me to work with them over the summer before automatically retaining them. They agreed, but with the condition that they would reassess their skills when school began. They warned me that if my sons could not meet second grade expectations that they would not be promoted on to the second grade.

It was then that I began my research on reading difficulties. I knew that I had to do something other than make my sons read more. Because the more I forced them to read, the more it made them, *and me*, anxious and frustrated. I found that there were no practical books for the proactive parent wanting to teach their child how to read, write, and spell. And even though I had found numerous books about dyslexia, they provided only vague descriptions of activities parents could do with their children. I wanted to know what activities truly fostered the skills needed when learning to read. I read several studies and decided that I would teach them phonics and in a way that made sense to me. I compiled the lessons, which later would evolve into my first instruction manual.

We worked hard that summer. And in the fall, the school reassessed my sons and they were both promoted on to the second grade. That school year, I continued to work with them and hired a reading tutor. She taught me how to effectively communicate with my children's teachers, counselor, and principal. She also inspired me to insist that a reluctant school assess my sons for dyslexia and to advocate for my children.

Even though I was certain they had dyslexia, their school (along with so many others back then) was in denial. I think back and remember how I felt when I realized that my sons had dyslexia. I was optimistic because knowing meant that I could finally find out what their true problems were and address the root causes of their issues. That gave me more peace than crossing my fingers and waiting for them to "mature" and for "the light bulb to come on." I could no longer bear their tears or hear my sons call themselves "stupid." I wanted them to know they had dyslexia and that their difficulties had nothing to do with how smart a person is or isn't. That was when Martha Hougen entered my life.

I called the school district and spoke with Dr. Martha Hougen who, at that time, was the Dyslexia Coordinator for Austin ISD. She listened carefully to how I described the specific difficulties they were having in school and what I felt the underlying causes were. I shared the specific types of activities that seemed to help and the ones that didn't. Afterwards, she personally saw to it that both my sons were screened.

After my sons were tested for dyslexia, their school could not provide them with intervention for dyslexia, so I offered to continue tutoring them myself at their school during school hours. I offered my services to other students as well. By the end of the year, I worked with 25 students at my sons' school and 9 others at a neighboring school. I recruited and trained 13 parent volunteers to tutor the 34 students. It was a grassroots, parent volunteer effort to support teachers in providing intervention to dyslexic students and other struggling readers. At the end of the year, I was awarded Volunteer of the Year by the school's PTA.

As other parents saw my children and student's successes, they asked if I could provide reading intervention to their children, so I began teaching students privately after school. I was exhilarated by my students' outcomes. My students became my heroes, and they inspired me to learn more, so I could help other struggling students become more competent and self-confident. I also worked part-time as a substitute teacher at two elementary schools.

In 2006, I went back to school and earned my Master's in Education (2008) from The University of Texas at Austin, specializing in Learning Disabilities and Behavioral Disorders. During my first year of coursework, I walked into a class, and guess who was my professor?

Dr. Martha Hougen, the person who gave me the confirmation that my sons had dyslexia. She inspired me to keep working with my sons, which lead me to becoming a reading tutor, authoring two instruction manuals, pursuing my Master's in Education, and formally testing my method of reading instruction on students with a variety of characteristics, such as dyslexia, ADHD, race, and economic status for my thesis. Dr. Hougen was an example of how one caring person can affect the lives of so many others.

While earning my Master's in Education at UT, my professor for my practicum assigned me to co-teach 6th grade Math during summer school. I asked my professor why she placed me in a math classroom when I knew so much about dyslexia. She said, "I want you to gain experience in math, so you can expand your knowledge and skills." I am forever grateful to her for that. Indeed, it did.

While teaching 6th grade Math, I learned how to treat deficits in mathematics and behaviors in the classroom. The students attending summer school were quite rowdy. Within the first few weeks, all summer school students were no longer allowed to eat in the cafeteria due to severe discipline problems. After students purchased their lunches, they had to return and eat in their classrooms. Not much later, all students needing to use the restroom would be required to walk with a designated escort to and from the restrooms. Our fellow teachers would mention their struggles to maintain learning environments. However, my co-teacher, Ms. Mireles, and I did not have a single power struggle, nor did we refer a student to the office, even though we had an active group with a variety of learning and behavioral challenges. I attribute our success to Ms. Mireles' knowledge of math interventions, our class structure and seating, and the lessons I provided. Every other day, I spent 15 minutes or less on what I called behavior empowerment lessons. I had previously created them for the students I privately tutored. I adapted them, so I could share them to my classroom of 6th graders and they are many of the lessons that can be found in each step of this book.

As fate would have it, my sons began to thrive and my daughter, Samantha, started having challenges in math. Two of her teachers had said that Samantha had the same characteristics as their students with ADHD. Her lack of focus, organization, and attention were preventing her from accomplishing tasks, such as memorizing her addition, subtraction, and multiplication facts, which in turn affected her division, multi-step, and word problems. I was able to collaborate with her wonderful teachers and together, we, were able to provide my daughter with the math instruction that addressed the root causes of her difficulties. In addition, we implemented academic and behavioral interventions to address her ADHD without medications. With time and practice self-monitoring, she began to thrive along with her brothers.

In 2009, my sons were in high school and doing so well that they wanted to help other students who were having difficulties reading. Preston and Warren understood what a difference reading intervention had made in their lives, and they wanted to help others.

They formally requested and founded a new club at their high school. They recruited fellow high school students to tutor and mentor middle school students (at their former middle school where their sister was attending, and I was PTA president). They hosted club meetings one day a week. I trained the students with games and fun activities on how to tutor and mentor students reading below grade-level. Twenty to 40 members attended the meetings and learned. The Covington Middle School principal and staff selected 18 students to be tutored. All the middle school students were either Limited English Proficient students, in Special Education, or identified with dyslexia. By the end of the school year, all the middle school students made gains in reading fluency and reading comprehension. The principal and staff were so appreciative of the high school tutors that they nominated them for and were awarded the Austin Voices for Education and Youth's *Shout Out Award* in 2010.

Over the years, I've fine-tuned my methods, and my private practice has expanded to teaching students of all abilities, perceptual styles, opportunities, and backgrounds. I have provided academic interventions for students, designed lessons, and differentiated instruction for students, pre-K through college and beyond. I've taught students who have dyslexia, dyscalculia, dysgraphia, ADHD, Autism, and orthographic processing deficits and students who are in Special Education, English Language Learner, and Gifted & Talented programs.

In 2014, I received a call from the assistant principal of a nearby middle school to teach an 8th grade English class as a permanent substitute teacher. One of her teachers was on maternity leave, and she expressed that she needed a teacher with my characteristics to teach that class. Something about the way she said it; I knew those students needed me. The job was for the remaining nine weeks of school. I hated the thought of temporarily putting the students I was privately teaching on hold, but it all somehow came together. And, it was meant to be.

During my first week at the middle school, a fight had broken out in the cafeteria and someone had pooped in the stairwell. There had been a sub for two weeks before I started teaching my class. Because of this, the students were way behind when I came into the classroom. On my third day, I printed out the grades for each of my class periods. In one period, all but four students were failing! My five other classes were slightly better off. After two solid weeks of following up with students, tutoring them, all but four passed that 6-weeks. I was very proud of them for coming to me for tutoring during their lunches and after school. My next priority was discipline, and I began my behavior empowerment lessons I shared with my 6th grader summer school class and are found in this book. I thank God that I did. It helped me start laying down some foundation my students would need to get through the next big hurdle. A tragedy.

My fourth week began with very sad news that an 8th grade student had committed suicide over the weekend. She was not a student of mine, but all my 8th grade students knew her and had been attending school with her over the years. The unexpected death of someone, especially under these circumstances, can bring out all kinds of emotions and behaviors within our young students. In the beginning, they all went through a period of shock, but it was no time before their feelings were manifested in classrooms, halls, gym, and cafeteria. It brought out tears, anger, spite, mischief, and deep depression in my students, and I had to help them get through all these emotions and behaviors that would randomly present themselves over the following weeks. It was during this experience as an 8th grade classroom teacher that I realized I had to finish this book and share it with others. Many of our schoolchildren may come across as apathetic or uncaring. Many may seem to lack a conscience. There's violence turning inward and outward. From that point onward, I've felt the need to share this very important message; you and I, we have the power to change the course of lives. We can improve our children and teen's mentalities, patterns, habits, and futures.

I have been on a journey that all started with my three biological children. My trek forged onward to include the children I've enjoyed teaching and learning from. I've witnessed my children and my students become more successful in their schools and homes. I've trained parent and student volunteers to work with students. I have also provided parent education to parents and professional development to classroom teachers. I've often served enthusiastically as a student and parent advocate. I've attended numerous parent-teacher conferences and assisted parents in advocating for their children. I have served the school community as a PTA president for five years. I've served multiple years as a member of the Campus Advisory Committee. All these experiences of being a parent, academic intervention tutor, classroom teacher, student/parent advocate, and PTA president have given birth to this book. I've been developing this book for over a decade. It has my DNA in it.

It's been quite a journey, and I have learned many lessons along the way. One of the most important is that just because a child struggles in school, it does not sentence him or her to a life of not being able to read, spell, write, calculate, communicate, comprehend, or motivate themselves. We can help the children and teens in our lives overcome their obstacles.

I believe that life *truly* is a journey and our destination is what we wish to accomplish during our journey. During my journey, the winds of life took me by surprise, and I had to begin my voyage before my ship had even been built. But I set my course, and it's been one heck of a ride. And dear reader, whether you know it or not, whether you're prepared or not, you've already set sail and your journey has already begun.

It was not easy to work with my own children; it was trying. But I can't think of anyone who is more worthy of my time, energy, and patience than my children. There is no greater purpose. I could see the big picture; how helping them would make a difference in our lives. It spurred me to take action and to keep going when I wanted to give up. The aperture expanded further to include the students I worked with in the classrooms and in my private practice. And now, I see an even bigger picture, and that picture includes you, dear reader.

However, my book is incomplete. You have to help me complete it with the journal opportunities at the end of each step. I haven't met your child or student. I could write about every type of child and every scenario and every solution for you and them. We don't have time for that. Besides, you know you and your student better than any author of any book. Each step of this book will provide you with lessons to contemplate and complete with your child or classroom. These will spur you to journal and share your stories, your wisdom, and your advice to yourself. I don't want to tell you what to do. I want you to tell yourself what to do. People can tell us what we're supposed to do, and we may or may not do it. However, if we tell ourselves what we should do, we are much more likely to, and we'll work with an elevated consciousness and thus experience more positive, rewarding outcomes.

Success will happen. And not because I tell you what to do, but because, you will journal it. You will tell yourself what to do to create the changes you want to see in your child or classroom.

This is our story. I've written my part. It's time for you to write yours.

STEP 1 | **CONTROL YOUR ANGER AND DISAPPOINTMENT**

WHEN THE GOING GETS TOUGH, IMAGINE SOMEONE IS RECORDING YOU

Sometimes our children and students will push us to our limits. It most often happens when failure is imminent. They shut down or won't listen, sometimes to the point we become anxious, panicked, or angry.

When we find ourselves losing patience, pretend someone is videotaping it. Ask yourself, "Would I be proud or embarrassed to view my behavior?" Martin Luther King, Jr. said, "The ultimate measure of a person is not where he or she stands in moments of comfort and convenience, but where he or she stands at times of challenge and controversy."

As caregivers we often neglect ourselves. However, we must nurture our bodies and minds, so we can do a better job nurturing our children. Reconnect with friends, exercise, or get massages regularly. We must do whatever it takes, so when they shut down or won't listen, we are less likely to lose our patience. We do not get a chance to rewind and re-record.

In the event we lose our patience and become angry, how can we reverse the damage? Letting time pass may work for some, but we run the risk that the person we hurt will stew over what was said and done. They may become resentful, rebellious, and defiant. At that point it can be much harder to earn their respect and cooperation.

Laughter, a hug, hearing someone say, "I'm sorry," creates biochemical changes in our brains and bodies. When we say we are sorry to someone, we can instantly see changes that occur on the outside of their bodies - their shoulders relax, their eyes soften, and their lips unpurse. Just imagine what happens biochemically inside their bodies as well.

Monkeys had overpopulated a village near a rain forest. A farmer cut holes in coconuts and filled them with fruit. If the monkeys put their hands in the coconut to get the yummy fruit, then they would not be able to pull their hands out and then the farmer could easily capture them. The monkeys wanted the fruit in the coconut so much that they couldn't let go of the fruit to climb up the trees.

Some people hold on to the pain and spite as though it were fruit and they can't let go. Likewise, we must also stop clinging to pain and anger as though they are fruit in a coconut.

We must LET GO, and forgive, and trust. Sometimes we think if we hold on to our resentment (fruit), then we will punish the people who've hurt us. But the only persons we're hurting are ourselves.

And if that's not enough, if we keep focusing on what we've lost, we'll lose what's left and miss out on what's to become of our future.

So, trust, have faith, and LIVE.

Author Unknown, Adapted by Laurie Hunter

We should be firm parents and strict teachers. We should stand our ground and insist they obey rules and work hard. However, when we're being strict and firm, we must show tact and grace. It takes a lot of strength to be a rigorous and ironclad parent or teacher. And if we lose our patience and apologize (without using the word "*but*")...that takes real strength and wielding of power. Over time, focus and grace will gain true respect, and our children will be more willing to do what we ask.

Lastly, when a child, student, spouse, family member, or friend has hurt you, whether they apologize to you or not, forgive them! Forgiveness is powerful. Forgiveness can release a person from jail. Think about all the thoughts you hold as prisoners within your body. You can free them. Forgive others and release the thoughts you are holding captive in your body.

Lesson 1 | The Fence
Author unknown, retold by Laurie Hunter

 Complete the following lesson with your child or students.
Instructor or parent reads:

There once was a boy with a temper. One day the boy's father gave him a box of nails and said, "Son, every time you lose your temper, I want you to hammer a nail into this fence." The boy drove 7 nails into the fence on that day.

In time the boy began to understand his anger and control his temper. Every day, the number of nails he hammered into the fence gradually decreased. He discovered it was better to control his temper than to drive nails into the fence.

As time passed, the boy realized it had been a long time since he lost his temper. He hadn't hammered a nail into to the fence for many weeks. He told his father about it. His father said, "I'm proud of you, Son. Now, you must pull out one nail each day you are able to control your temper."

Days passed and the young boy was finally able to tell his father that all the nails had been pulled out of the fence.

On that day, the father said, "My son, look at all the holes in the fence. The nails of your anger have pierced this fence, and the fence will never be the same again. Your next task is to always remember this fence before you become angry. When you say angry words, hit, or push people, those actions leave scars in the people you've hurt, just like your nails have left scars in this fence."

Journal 1 | Kick-Start Respect

 Instructor or parent journals:

Reflect about a time in your life when you became angry and took it out on someone else. Write down what made you so angry that you hurt someone else? Was it because you were exhausted, going through a divorce, someone let you down, or your pet died?

Next, think about when you became angry or spoke disrespectfully to your child or student. Was it because you were worn out, tired, or overwhelmed? Or, did something bad happen? Did you get a speeding ticket, miss lunch, or have an argument with someone? What could you have done to prevent yourself from getting angry? If someone had videotaped you, would you have been proud or embarrassed? How could you have spoken with more grace and tact?

Now, think about how your child or a student is being disrespectful to you. Think about what may be going on in your student or child's life. You don't know if their parents had a fight or are going through a divorce. For all you know, their parent may be in jail or their dog may have died. Our students experience some of the same things we do. However, they lack the maturity and skills to deal with what's going on in their lives. No matter how disrespectful they may be to you, you don't know what's going on in their life. And, that's why we should never assume a child is simply disrespectful without a reason. There is *always* an underlying cause for why they are reacting unfavorably to you. Write down reasons why you feel he or she is unable to treat you with respect. How could you act with more grace? Reacting angrily only puts more holes in the fence. How could you prevent making new scars?

The purpose of Step 1 is not about getting the respect we deserve from our children or students. We will cultivate respect with the completion of each unit in this book. Rather, the purpose of Step 1 is to reduce the shame and affliction that anger can create in our homes and classrooms. It may be helpful to remember that our children haven't had the years of training and experience we've had. They are developing the skills to cope with adversity and frustration, and we are a part of that process. So when they feel shame, it may make them angry and behave unfavorably. When we, parents and teachers, are oblivious or do not understand, we may retaliate by being angry or sarcastic back. Over time, this can incubate power struggles and rebelliousness. This journal is about finding the grace when frustrations escalate to prevent us from adding more holes in the fence.

LAURIE HUNTER

STEP 2 | PRACTICE USING LANGUAGE THAT MOTIVATES

DO WHATEVER IT TAKES TO REMAIN POSITIVE

What's the difference between driving your child into the ground and driving your child to do his or her best? The answer is inspiration. Inspiration will motivate, fuel determination, and increase the success of a struggling student. Can you inspire someone by yelling at them? When was last time you were inspired by someone repeatedly yelling at you?

To inspire your child, you must transform your negative language to a positive and affirming language. By language, I mean your body language, tone of voice, and choice of words.

Figure 2.1   Body Language and Tone Convey 93% (Albert Mehrabian)

55%	Of every message is communicated through body language.
38%	Of every message is communicated through the tone of your voice.
7%	Of every message is communicated through your words.

I stop at a red light and glance at the mini-van next to me. The driver appears to be a mother of her two children sitting still in the back seat. The woman has a severe and harsh look on her face. How can I tell what she's thinking when I'm not speaking with her? I can tell, because her body language is communicating nonverbally. Without saying a word to me, she "told" me how dissatisfied and disdainful she is feeling.

Albert Mehrabian made significant contributions in the field of nonverbal communication. His findings have helped us understand how humans express and nonverbally communicate things such as hierarchy, uneasiness, insecurity, empathy, anger, and deception in our behaviors. Since body language and tone of voice can convey these, it's important not to take these two elements for granted. Instead, we should *actively* monitor and carefully choose our words, tone, and body language. When we convey our feelings and attitudes more respectfully, we can leave a lasting positive impression.

COMMUNICATE YOUR BELIEF, EVEN IF YOU DON'T

By focusing on the positive and communicating our belief in a child, we help them see potential they may not be aware of. I agree with Henry Ford who said, "If you think you can, or think you can't...you're right!" Ford and other inventors could "see" and believed in what could be. Sometimes, we only need to think we can. Similarly, when we, teachers and parents, maintain positive focus, communication, and belief in our children and teens, it is only a matter of time before they will begin to see and believe.

It is our job as parents and teachers to push our children past their challenges and to push them beyond, "I can't" so they reach their fullest potential. It is an encouraging and reassuring push to promote an "I can" attitude. They need to believe they have the ability (self-efficacy). It is a push that expects a high level of self-discipline, goal planning, and hard work. Dear parents and teachers, those of you who can support these needs will have a powerful effect on your children.

As an adult woman, Lisa Fittipaldi became blind. She was unable to see color, dimension, or print. In 1995, two years after she lost her vision, Lisa learned how to paint. She developed her own way of painting complex, realistic scenes. When looking at her paintings, you may wonder how a blind person could possibly paint so well?

So, what does a blind painter have to do with your child or students? Everything. Lisa does not use the same method to paint as a painter who can see. One may think that she does not have what is necessary to paint realistic works of art. You may think, right now, your child or students will never respect or cooperate with you. Dear reader, behaviorally and academically challenged children can learn too.

Children must know they *truly* have the power to achieve. As parents, teachers, tutors, mentors, and coaches, it's important we search for the *potential that may not be easily seen* in our children and students. We can help them "see" and *realize* the potential within themselves.

Frequently communicating your belief in your child's potential through your body language, tone of voice, and words is an investment. "It's a relatively small investment with incalculable, unbelievable results. Again, remember the incredible effect it has upon us when someone communicates his or her belief in us (our potential) when we don't believe in ourselves (our history)" (Covey, 2004, p 73).

"Seeing people through the lens of their potential and their best actions, rather than through the lens of their current behavior or weaknesses, generates positive energy and reaches out and embraces others. This affirming action is also one of the keys to rebuilding broken relationships... When we perceive and acknowledge the potential of others, it is as if we hold up a mirror to them reflecting the best within them" (Covey, 2004, p 72-73).

For instance, "When we look at a few examples of highly successful dyslexics and visual thinkers, we can see that they have many strengths that are often not properly recognized in school but come to be recognized in work and in life. Seeing the longer-term implications—in spite of tradition—we become aware that we need to find ways of seeing and developing the gifts and talents hidden under the difficulties. When we look at highly successful individuals, we see that they succeeded by following their substantial gifts, not by focusing on their difficulties" (West, 1997, p 264).

What about the children and teens who are annoying, rude, or making bad choices? And, what about the ones who seem so full of themselves and bully others? Do we communicate our belief in them? It is even more important that parents and teachers make an effort. Annoying and undesirable behaviors stem from some root cause. How do you know if someone is physically, sexually, or emotionally abusing them? Or that someone in their family has been battling cancer or an addiction or family violence? Maybe their parents are going through a divorce? When our children and teens become so annoying or rude, try to refrain from judging, and I challenge you to put the ideas in this book to the test.

SEARCH FOR YOUR CHILD'S HIDDEN POTENTIAL

Parents and teachers of children with dyslexia, ADHD, dysgraphia, speech, vision, and hearing impairments, autism, OCD, and behavior disorders will benefit from understanding children's strengths and weaknesses. As a result, weaknesses can be addressed, and strengths can be fostered. Is there some unseen potential skill or talent you can help your child or student realize? If you don't see it now, be patient, because at some point you will. Meanwhile, he or she will need your encouragement and support to develop those strengths, even if you wonder if it will ever happen.

COMMUNICATE HOW WEAKNESSES CAN BECOME STRENGTHS

It is well documented that people with dyslexia, ADHD, OCD, autism, etc. develop giftedness in some skill. If your child struggles in any area, collect facts, stories, and examples of people who have overcome similar struggles. However, if your child or student doesn't have a specific learning difference, then find stories and facts about people who have overcome odds and how their weaknesses became strengths. Good examples are Abraham Lincoln, Thomas Edison, Wilma Rudolph, and Wendy Booker.

Children who lack respect and cooperation may have an underlying learning disability or they may be experiencing stress or trauma you're not aware of. They may become restless, start talking, act out, or even make fun of you. Please note, they need to hear how other people have overcome their struggles just as much as the children sitting quietly next to them. Stirring hope motivates children to achieve cooperation, respect, and success. You can be firm and strict and still deliver your message in a caring and inspirational manner.

Example

If difficulties associated with learning challenges aren't addressed, they can affect self-confidence, classroom behaviors, and emotional wellbeing. The following example shows information a teacher or parent could compile and share with children who have learning differences. I chose dyslexia, since it affects about 20% of schoolchildren.

The classroom teacher begins by saying how 1 in 5 students has dyslexia. He says, "Today, I would like to talk about dyslexia. Dyslexia is a difficulty with language that makes it challenging to learn how to read, spell, and express thoughts in writing. However, many students with dyslexia learn and use strategies to overcome these difficulties. Today I would like to talk about the *benefits* associated with dyslexia. Many people know about the difficulties, but not the positive aspects."

The teacher continues by explaining that people with dyslexia differ in how they process information; therefore, their perceptions of the world are different. Because of this, they often approach problems with different perspectives. And this often leads them to discover unique, original solutions and authentic responses. Dyslexics often develop intelligence, strengths, talents, and skills in problem solving.

Dyslexics have an advantage in coming up with creative, novel approaches to situations and solving problems. This is shown by their high representation in the top levels of art, science, and business fields. This is possibly due to differences in how their minds are wired. Dyslexics approach problems and solutions from new angles, and they can become quite talented in solving problems. This arduous process can create significant advantages over one-track, linear, sequential thinkers (Gorman, 2003, p 54).

In *Overcoming Dyslexia*, Dr. Shaywitz comments, "dyslexics appear to be disproportionately represented in the upper echelons of creativity and in the people who, whether in business, finance, medicine, writing, law, or science, have broken through a boundary and have made a real difference to society. I believe this is because a dyslexic cannot simply memorize or do things by rote; she must get far underneath the concept and understand it at a fundamental level. This need often leads to a deeper understanding and a perspective that is different from what is achieved by some for whom things come easier because they just can memorize and repeat—without ever having to deeply and thoroughly understand" (Shaywitz, 2003, p 57).

Another source asserts, "If we could somehow prevent these brain changes, and thus prevent the appearance of dyslexia, might we not find that we have deprived the society of an important and irreplaceable group of individuals endowed with remarkable talents?" (West, 1997, p 23)

Dyslexia didn't stop these famous men and women from achieving greatness:

Scientists	Einstein, Thomas Edison, Stephen Hawking, Kettner Griswold, Niels Bohr, Michael Faraday, Alexander Graham Bell, Jack Horner
Leaders	Erin Brockovich, Winston Churchill, General Patton
Innovative Business Entrepreneurs	Steve Jobs, Henry Ford, Nelson Rockefeller, Charles Schwab, William Hewlett (Hewlett-Packard), Ted Turner (Turner Broadcasting)
Movie visionaries	Steven Spielberg, Walt Disney
Authors	Patricia Pollacco, Dav Pilkey, Earnest Hemmingway, John Grisham, Hans Christian Anderson, Agatha Christie, F. Scott Fitzgerald, Laurie Hunter
Artists	Leonardo da Vinci, Michelangelo, Rodin, Ansel Adams
Explorers	Charles Lindbergh, Ann Bancroft
Athletes	Terry Bradshaw, Nolan Ryan, Tim Tebow, Magic Johnson
Singers	Jewel, Cher, Joss Stone
Comedians	Jay Leno, Robin Williams
Actors	Tom Cruise, George Clooney, James Earl Jones, Whoopi Goldberg, Channing Tatum, Keira Knightly, Orlando Bloom

The teacher concluded, "We cannot neglect the idea that many kinds of intelligences exist. Indeed, memorizing facts by rote is one type of intelligence. But, so is the intelligence required to create the brilliant scientific and artistic works of dyslexic Leonardo da Vinci. We cannot deny the intelligence required of Winston Churchill. His dyslexia did not prevent him from inspiring nations to stand up and fight Hitler. What would Europe look like today without the strength and intelligence of Winston Churchill? Today, we are focusing on how our world needs people with dyslexia. Our world needs people from all different backgrounds, experiences, skills, communication styles, and learning differences. It's what makes our world spin."

Lesson 2 | Purple and Blue: Valuing Differences
Bryan Fiese, adapted by Laurie Hunter

 Complete the following lesson with your child or students to show why we should all focus on the positive.
Instructor or parent reads:

Let's explore why it's important to focus on the positive. Humor me by participating in a 20-second activity. Look around the room. Look for everything that is purple in the room. Keep looking all around for things that are purple for about 10 more seconds.

Let's see if you can close your eyes and try to remember everything that was purple. Close your eyes and think of everything that was purple.

Keep your eyes closed, but now try to recall everything that was blue. Keep your eyes closed!

Now open your eyes. Why is it hard remembering what was blue? It was hard to remember what was blue because we were focusing on the purple; we were looking for the purple and that's what we remembered. The same thing happens when we continually focus on the negative. We will remember the bad, and neglect seeing the positive.

Let's take a vow to search for and focus on the positive, especially when times are hard.

Journal 2 | Kick-Start Motivation by Staying Positive

 Instructor or parent journals:

Reflect on the times you are most negative. What are some ways you can remain positive when communicating with your child or student? (e.g. find the blessing in the situation, spend time with friends and family who are positive forces). What and where could you post something in your home or classroom as a reminder of what you will do when you start to become negative?

What strengths does he or she possess? How will you foster his or her strengths? If you're not sure, pay close attention. Over time, those strengths *will* inevitably be revealed to you. What are your child's weaknesses? How could they turn into strengths or blessings? (e.g. By taking my child to tutoring and constantly staying positive. Because of my child's _____, he will have to work harder than his classmates and, over time, he will develop a better work ethic than his peers.)

What are some things you can do to keep your child or student positive? How can you improve your body language and tone? How can you prevent yourself from saying clichés and speak with more authenticity and a positive attitude?

Attitudes

The longer I live, the more I realize the importance
of choosing the right attitude in life.
Attitude is more important than facts.
It is more important than your past;
more important than your education or financial situation;
more important than your circumstances, your successes, or your failures;
more important than what other people think, say or do.
It is more important than your appearance, your giftedness, or your skills.
It will make or break a company. It will cause a church to soar or sink.
It will make the difference between a happy home or a miserable home.
You have a choice each day regarding the attitude you will embrace.

Life is like a violin.
You can focus on the broken strings that dangle,
or you can play your life's melody on the one that remains.
You cannot change the years that have passed,
nor can you change the daily tick of the clock.
You cannot change the pace of your march toward your death.
You cannot change the decisions or the reactions of other people.
And you certainly cannot change the inevitable.
Those are the strings that dangle!
What you can do is play on the one string that remains – your attitude.
I am convinced that life is 10 percent what happens to me
and 90 percent how I react to it.
The same is true for you.

STEP 3 | ASK FOR COOPERATION

SAY WHAT'S IN IT FOR THEM

Our children and students need to see the big picture in order to cooperate. They must learn how making good grades and choices will truly make a difference in their lives. We are more successful in reaching a goal when we understand the meaning and purpose for achieving that goal. Why is that? Because once we understand the purpose, then we begin to *make better choices and take action in our daily lives.* In turn, each passing day will bring us closer to accomplishing our goal.

Also, children and students need to see the bigger picture in order to maintain their respect while we push them towards their potential. Repeatedly, I would explain to my children, "It is my job to be the best parent I can be, and I take my job seriously. It is my job to ensure that you do your best and grow into productive, valuable, and contributing members in the world. I have a lot to accomplish in your short 18 years with me. I need your cooperation." Likewise, I tell my students that they are like my children, and I want to share as much as I can with them during our limited time together. Don't think you need to say this to your students, especially if you wouldn't mean it.

If you want their cooperation in the classroom or during homework, it is imperative to share the big picture - why school is important. And to be most effective, you must include what's in it for them.

Lesson 3 | More Playtime Later

 Complete the following lesson with your child or students to highlight the importance of education and what it can do for them.
Instructor or parent reads:

Someone can take your lunch money, your book, or your clothes. But, can you think of something that no one can steal from you? There aren't many things that cannot be taken away. Can anyone steal your education?

Do you know why teachers and parents get mad at you when you don't do well in school? Because, we are trying to give you something valuable, something that no one can take away from you, and you're fighting us by goofing off or not listening. Help me (and your teachers) give you something that no one else can steal.

The main reason education is so valuable is because it's something you can have that no one can take away from you. If someone takes your diploma, your achievement will always exist. Can you think of another reason why getting an education is so important?

When I was younger, it was possible to get a job that required little schooling but paid well. For instance, construction (e.g. road, house) and manufacturing (e.g. car, clothing, toys, furniture) were jobs that paid well for people who did not go to college. Unfortunately, it is almost impossible to pay the bills without a college education today.

Take a look at the following visual. It can help us understand the importance of getting your high school diploma. It shows us how going to college greatly increases your chances of making more money in life.

Figure 3.1   Yearly Earnings Increase with Educational Attainment

Professional Degree	$87,400
Master's Degree	$60,700
Bachelor's Degree	$49,600
Associate's Degree	$36,600
High School Diploma	$28,700
No High School Diploma	$20,300

The 2012 U.S. Census Bureau data shows that yearly earnings increase with education.
Adults 25 and over who did not graduate from high school earned a median income of $20,300 per year.
Adults 25 and over that graduated from high school made a median income of $28,700 per year.
The median income for adults 25 and older, who earned an Associate Degree, made $36,900 per year.
Those who had a Bachelor's Degree made $49,600; Master's Degree made $60,700; and Professional Degree earned $87,400 per year.
(U.S. Census Bureau, 2012, Table Pinc-03)

How much money do adults 25 and over make if they do not graduate from high school? How much more can you make if you graduate?

How much more money can you make with a college education? I'm not saying that if you go to college you will automatically be rich. Nor am I saying that if you don't go to college you can't be rich. It can happen.

But, now do you see why you should strive for the best grades possible?

However, it's not just about being rich or making enough money to live comfortably either. Money may not be important to everyone. So, let's see what else could be more important.

What are some things you like to do during your playtime? (One said play video games, another said spend time with my family, and another said go on vacation.)

> (Write down their responses, "video games, family, vacations...")

Is playtime important to you? Well, you know what? I think playtime is important too. (Pause) But, I am less concerned with how much playtime you have *now*. I'm *much more* concerned with how much playtime you will have *when you're 30*. (Productive Pause) Thirty is a long way away. Why should you care now? Let me show you.

Everyone lives in a home or an apartment. Sometimes we have hard times and have to live in a car or a shelter. But, think about where you would like to live. We all have to pay money to live somewhere. I paid $1400 every month to live in my one-story home with a small yard. Let's say your home or apartment costs $1000/mo.

To pay for your home, what's a *good* job you could have that doesn't require an advanced degree? (Someone may say working as a cashier at the grocery store or working in a fast food restaurant.)

Those are good, respectable jobs that wouldn't require an advanced degree. How much do you think you could make per hour? (They may have no clue.)

People working jobs, such as these, typically start out making $10 an hour. Let's just say you're a cashier at a grocery store and you're making $10 an hour.

Now tell me, how many hours will you have to work to pay for your home if you make $10 an hour? (Calculate) $1000 divided by $10 equals 100 hours. So, you would have to work 100 hours a month to pay for your house, right?

> Write down, "**Job 1 $10/hour x 100 hours = $1000**"

But, you know what? With a college education and a few years of work experience, people, as smart as you, can make $40 an hour or more by the time they are 30. Now, let's say you're making $40 an hour, how many hours do you have to work to pay for your $1,000/month home? (Calculate) Let's see, $1000 divided by $40 equals 25 hours. So, you would have to work 25 hours to pay for your house.

> Write down, "Job 2 $40/hour x 25 hours = $1000"

Now tell me, which job will give you more playtime? (Allow for a productive pause.)

Point out the difference in the number of hours:

Job 1 $10/hour x 100 hours = $1000

Job 2 $40/hour x 25 hours = $1000

Would you rather work **25** hours or **100** hours to live in your simple home? (Allow for a productive pause.)

Which job would give you more time? Job 2 provides 75 more hours of your time to play with your family, go on vacation, and play video games. (Allow for a "huh" or "oh, I never thought of it *that way* before.")

You see, it's not just about money. More importantly, it's about having more time to do things you enjoy.

So, let's review. Why is it important to do well in school and get a good education? (Give them a chance to respond, and then say the following.)

A high school diploma and college degree are things that no one can take away from you. The more education, the more likely you are to make more money. And the more education/money you have, the more playtime you'll have. So, it's not just about making money; it's more about having the time to do the things you enjoy.

Do you know why else I want you to make a lot of money? Because the world has a lot of people with a lot of money who may not necessarily do good things with their money. The world needs people with good hearts, like you, to make a lot of money and do good things with it.

Lesson 3 continued | Explain the Importance of Self Control

 Instructor or parent reads:

What is self-control? (Controlling yourself) Self-control is *you* controlling *your* body.

Why is that important? (Allow for a productive pause.)

Because, if you can't control yourself, who do you think will?

Do you realize if you can't control yourself, your teacher will try to control you? (Productive pause)

If you can't control your actions, then your teacher, your school, and I will control you. Everyone must learn and practice self-control, and I know you can do it. I expect it, because I know how capable you are. Is there some way I can help? What can I do?

Journal 3 | Positively Motivate Students to Do Better in School

 Instructor or parent journals:

Save the notes you wrote down during Lesson 3 More Playtime Later. Keep it handy so you can pull it out in the future to remind them why doing well in school is important. Reflect on how the conversation might go. Write down clichés you will avoid.

Write down how you can explain that working hard and doing well in school is not only about making a lot of money. It's about having something no one else can take away, as well as making enough income so we can have the time to do the things we enjoy.

STEP 4 | **START BUILDING SELF-EFFICACY**

BEFORE YOU CAN CULTIVATE CONFIDENCE, YOU MUST BUILD SELF-EFFICACY

When something bad happens, what is it that makes some people think and feel like they can rise above their challenges, while others want to give up in defeat? It's called self-efficacy. People who believe in their abilities to rise above tasks or challenges have a good sense of self-efficacy. Strong self-efficacy makes reaching a goal more likely and leads to *true* self-confidence.

In contrast, people who lack belief in their abilities to overcome situations have a poor sense of self-efficacy. Hence, they don't really believe they are capable, and they lose faith in their abilities. If not addressed, this can lead to the development of poor self-confidence.

Keep in mind, just because someone does not feel capable in *one* area of their life, it does not mean that he or she will have a poor sense of efficacy in *every* aspect of life. It is untrue and disempowering to believe someone could be deficient in every way. Every person is capable in *some* aspect(s). For instance, one may doubt his or her abilities in mathematics but may feel competent in maintaining relationships at home.

For decades, researchers and psychologists have shown that self-efficacy can impact goal achievement in education, health, athletic and musical performance, addictions, etc. The key for us, parents and educators, is to acknowledge the relationships that exist between self-efficacy and academic success and address them.

Address self-efficacy in as many ways as you can.

- Assist the student in setting goals (see Step 6 Set Goals that Will Increase Self-Confidence and Step 7 Monitor Goals).
- Explain that a person cannot reach a destination in a single step. Ask the student to imagine walking from one side of the room to the other in one step. Explain how every journey is made up of many steps and we cannot reach our destination in the first step.
- Frequently comment on successes *privately* to children. Some students may live to stand out and receive compliments publicly. However, many children do not want parents or teachers to draw attention to them in front of others, even when they

are successful. Many times, private communication can be more meaningful, and powerful, to inspire a child in a family and classroom.

- Periodically, rejoice and reward accomplishments to every family member or student in the classroom. Think of it in the same way as an employer organizing an end-of-quarter party. The host reviews team or company goals and celebrates how everyone came together to accomplish those goals. It is a morale-boosting event that makes everyone feel appreciated and rewarded. It's not a time to call anyone out or to give specific recognition to a few people. Doing so would disenfranchise an employee. It would have a similar effect in a family or classroom. That's why it's important to rejoice and reward everyone periodically.
- Collect students' work and give them opportunities to review their progress in motivating ways.

Prevent feelings of failure to maintain and preserve self-efficacy.

- Don't ask a student to go too far beyond his or her ability.
- Don't skip steps. If you think something will be too easy, have the student go through it anyway. If it is easy then it won't take much of your time and, most importantly, it will build confidence.

If the student fails, restore his or her self-efficacy.

- Respect the student's dignity.
- Quickly follow up by placing them in a situation you know they will succeed.
- Establish the FACT that we all learn from our mistakes.

Difficulties in school and/or at home take a toll on self-efficacy. Encouragement and support should be provided to every student, whether or not we think they are experiencing challenges. Just because students haven't told us their story, it doesn't mean they don't have one. Many students work very hard to hide academic or social difficulties and roadblocks. Also, some are secretly dealing with parental neglect, incarceration, depression, family violence, divorce, abuse, or other traumatic events.

Children and teenagers are still developing the skills to cope with academic, social, and emotional realities. Their pain may manifest as inattention or rebellion. They may appear as though they are not trying, or it may seem they are being difficult on purpose. These are signs that something could be troubling them, even if they are in middle and high school.

At times you may be so certain nothing is wrong and find yourself thinking, "Why shouldn't I put this child in his place and teach him a lesson?" You may be right. But, what if you're not? Think about what happens when you put down a child. It might make you feel better temporarily. And, you might make him or her an example to the other students in the classroom. But, ask yourself, "What does it do to the minds of the children you put down?"

It communicates to them that they are not good enough. It humiliates them, it breaks their trust, and they will not respect you.

I'm asking you to look beyond what your eyes are seeing and your ears are hearing. You can do this by asking yourself, "Why is this kid being such a snot?" Remain calm and say to yourself, "This child must be experiencing something awful I'm not aware of."

Teachers can privately ask their students to see them at the end of class. Begin by asking them what's going on. Tell them, "Your behavior was unacceptable in class, so I'm thinking something must be wrong. A happy student, who has everything going for them, does not act like you did today. Are you okay? Is something wrong?" That might be enough for them to tell you. If they maintain that nothing is wrong, then tell them, "If you ever need to talk about anything, I will be there for you."

I'm not telling you to turn a blind eye to their misbehaviors or to deny them of feeling consequences for their wrongdoings. Always give consequences and follow through. But, do it in a caring manner. How? Tell them flat out, "If I let you get away with this, am I doing you a favor? Not at all. Instead, I would be doing the opposite."

Above all, increase your awareness of your body language (e.g. scowling, narrowing of your eyes), choice of words (e.g. you're so irresponsible, why can't you...), and punitive actions (active and passive aggressive punishments). These damage children's self-efficacy. Negative body language, words, and actions make children feel like whatever they do, it will not make a difference. By stomping on them, you may gain temporary control and results. But, you are not making your life easier. Instead, you are waging a battle with the price of a child's future. Is that really worth it?

When your children or students struggle academically, behaviorally, or socially and make mistakes, restrain yourself from using negative methods. Instead, give corrective feedback by telling them what they are doing wrong. As a result, they can see and learn from the errors they make. Not in an "I told you so" way, but rather *in the most positive manner.*

I am dyslexic. One of my first memories is when I was in first grade. Another teacher came into the classroom to teach me how to read. Most people were too young to remember learning to read. But, I was old enough to remember. Later, when I was in fourth grade, my neighbor and I would play school. I remember thinking to myself, "Hum...I think I would like to be a teacher. But, I will never be a reading teacher." At the time, I hated reading. I had been a failure at it. You see, I had made mistake after mistake and it was hard work. It had taken its toll on my self-efficacy, self-confidence, self-esteem, and all the other selfs!

Ironically, here's where the story takes a twist. That same year, I had a reading teacher, Mrs. Desha. She taught me phonics and she was patient. She began the restoration of my self-efficacy in reading and spelling. As fortune would have it, the following year of fifth grade, I had Mrs. Martin. She pointed out my errors in the most positive manner and complimented me privately on my progress. In turn, she expanded my self-efficacy in reading, spelling, and handwriting. In high school, I had Mrs. Marilyn Wooldridge for 10th and 11th grade. She helped me develop the skills and, more importantly, my "can do" attitude in written expression. These three teachers are largely responsible for why you are reading this right now. Whether you are a teacher, tutor, or a parent helping your child do homework, will you be a Mrs. Desha, Mrs. Martin, or a Mrs. Wooldridge?

Because of my adversity and three encouraging teachers, my abilities, confidence, and work ethic increased, turning what once was a weakness into a strength. Years ago, I captured this sentiment in my journal.

Journal 8-31-04
To Be Dyslexic

Because of the wind, a young tree grows stronger.
I am like the young tree that is tossed by the wind.
And so as I sway in the winds of life, my inner core is strengthened.
And as I bend in the forceful winds, I will build a precious reservoir of strength.

Laurie Hunter

What if the wind is too forceful for your child or student?

I believe the spirit of a child is tenacious. And, isn't it true that the challenges of life can bring out the best in us? But, at what point do hardship, adversity, and failure interfere with a positive self-image and take its toll on a child's confidence and self-efficacy? What is the breaking point?

Some students must work harder than their classmates to keep up and experience failure more often. How can someone who falls behind and fails repeatedly build a healthy work ethic and positive attitude?

The restoration, maintenance, and preservation of self-esteem and confidence of a struggling child is essential. An encouraging person can help a child that loses spirit recover. It can not only help them survive the tumultuous winds of life, but also fortify their inner cores and build precious reservoirs of courage and strength. A child or teen who is failing can tap into their supply, so they will keep trying, learn from their mistakes, and develop their belief that one day they will become more competent.

Lesson 4 | When They Make Mistakes, Say This...

Complete the following lesson with your child or students when you feel they are embarrassed from making a mistake.
Instructor or parent reads:

You know, just because you made a mistake, it doesn't mean you're not smart. I know how smart you are.

It's a fact; smart people, like us, make mistakes all the time. When we learn we did something wrong and understand why we goofed, it helps us not make the same mistake again. That's what makes a smart person smart.

So, when you realize you've made a mistake, don't get embarrassed. Instead, realize we all make mistakes. Evaluate what you did wrong, and give it another try, and ask for help if you need it.

Journal 4 | Kick-Start Self-Efficacy

Instructor or parent journals:

Think about when and where your child or student makes mistakes that upsets them most. Write down ideas and think about what you will say to them. The following may help stimulate ideas.

People who are viewed as unsuccessful in the classroom are likely to repeatedly make mistakes. Over time, they begin to view themselves as incompetent. A parent or teacher can address this at any time; it is never too late.

Will you be a Mrs. Desha (the first person who has an effect - a restorer), a Mrs. Martin (someone in the middle - a maintainer), or a Mrs. Wooldridge (a final polish - a preserver)?

Write down who and how you will help. Specifically, think of ways you may be stripping children or teens of their dignity.

How will you assert they are smart? Remember, people who are "smart" recognize their mistakes, study why they made them, and make conscious efforts to not make them again. And, if it takes asking someone for help, the "smart" person will have the courage to ask.

STEP 5 | GUIDE THEM TO MAKE GOOD CHOICES

EXPLAIN LIFE IS A SERIES OF CHOICES

Sometimes people do not have the life they wanted. They can be so unhappy and not understand where they went wrong. Many times, bad things just happen - things they couldn't have avoided and that pushed them farther from the grades, job, or family life they wanted. Once you've completed Steps 5, 6, 7, and 10 regarding goals, it will be easier to explain to your children or students how life is a series of events that involve choices, decisions, and taking action that can get us closer to having the lives we want.

After the following lesson, briefly explain how our lives are less ruled by good and bad luck, and more by a *series* of choices. Indeed, bad things can happen, but if we work on reaching our goals, little by little, our lives begin to take shape in the direction we chose. The key to making that happen lies in focusing our energy on our priorities.

Lesson 5 | The 4 Rocks

For this activity you will need a jar, 4 rocks, and small pretty pebbles. Make sure you practice the following lesson before you present it to your child or classroom of students. During this lesson you will create a 3-D visual to display in the home or classroom that will represent the importance of putting our priorities first. Over time, you can point to it as a visual reminder when needed.
Instructor or parent reads the information on the left below:

See these 4 rocks. Each rock represents four of the most important things in your life. What are the most important things in your life?

Take a few guesses. What are the 4 most important things in your life?

- Should you put your family before friends?
- What about your school, job, and career?
- What helps you get through hard times? God, religion, faith, or hope?
- Is your health more important than most things?

The four most important things to you might be different from me and someone else.

But let's say these four big rocks represent family, school, faith, and health.

And these small pebbles over here represent the less important things, like clothes.

Should clothes or video games come before family? No, that's why they are pebbles.

Some of you may question whether you should have a big rock representing God, religion, faith, or hope. I think so, and here's why. Imagine you're going through your deepest, darkest time. What could help you get through it? Is it prayer? Or is it faith that it will all be okay? Or is it your hope that you'll get through the sadness? I'm sorry to tell you this, but we will all go through hard times during our lives. Which one of these could help you get through your pain: hope, faith, religion, or God? Pick one you are comfortable with and figure out how you can develop it, so when you're feeling low and suffering, you will have something that can help you. And don't let anyone take it away! Figure out which one can help prevent despair from setting in. Pick one that's right for you and make it a priority.

Pour the pebbles into the jar.

What if I wanted to put my 4 big rocks in this jar? Can I?

Try to put them in the jar and show how they won't fit.

Pour all the rocks out so that the jar is empty again.

Now remember each of these rocks symbolize what we said are most important. They are our priorities. And this time I'm going to put them into the jar first.

In life, if you're making a decision and you put the important things first, it's like putting these rocks in this jar.

Pour the small pebbles over the big rocks so they can see how they all fit.

It's the same in real life. If you put the big rocks in first there will be plenty of room for the little things. However, if you fill your jar with the little, insignificant things in life first, you won't have room for what is really important in life.

So, how can we make our family, school, faith, and health are our priorities? How can we put them first? We can by making decisions and choices in those 4 areas first. And when we do, everything else will come together.

Journal 5 | Putting the Big Rocks First

 Instructor or parent journals:

Reflect on what could be the "little" pebbles that might be preventing you from focusing on your 4 "big" rocks. Write about at least one. How is your attention to minor things diverting you from attending to your 4 "big" rocks and possibly hurting you or someone else? Write ideas about how you can stop putting that little rock in the jar before the big ones.

STEP 6 | SET GOALS THAT WILL INCREASE SELF-CONFIDENCE

CULTIVATE SELF-CONFIDENCE

If you want cooperation and respect, you may wonder why you should help children and teens set academic, athletic, and artistic goals. Making students set goals pertaining only to their behaviors shows that you care about you. Helping them set and reach their personal goals shows them you care about their well-being. When children sense you care about their hopes and dreams, they will care more about how they treat you.

As a parent, teacher, coach, counselor, or tutor, you can start goal planning by asking your child or student what he or she would like to see happen (the goal) and why (the motivation). The words must come out of their mouths. We guide them. We write down their goals. Then, we help them develop motivation and determination to achieve their goals. We help them identify actions, decisions, and choices that will take them closer to reaching their goals.

We encourage them to practice, even though it is hard, because skill, ability, knowledge, and understanding can only be gained through practice. Some students must work harder than their classmates. There's no way around it. For them, you may have to frequently proclaim the blessings that stem from pushing through pain. For example, students who face immense obstacles, but are encouraged as children can become hard working, perseverant, and resilient adults. In contrast, when school comes naturally for children, they may not develop a robust work ethic until later in life. Students who are challenged early on, but receive support, encouragement, and patience, will develop a vigorous work ethic. Isn't it true that when you exercise, you are making the heart work harder? Yet by making the heart work harder, it becomes stronger and healthier. It is when we challenge our hearts, our bodies, and our minds that we become stronger and healthier.

When they accomplish each goal, check it off together and celebrate. Think about a time when you said to yourself that you would do something courageous. Really, think of a time when you put yourself out there. When you achieved a seemingly impossible goal, didn't you feel a surge of confidence? They need to feel the thrill and euphoria from saying, "I did it!" Likewise, by celebrating the attainment of one small goal after another, their self-efficacy will strengthen, and their confidence will grow.

Before you set goals with your child or students, they will be more likely to reach them if they understand how confidence is derived. They need to understand that people are not born with confidence and that neither you nor anyone else can give it to them.

Lesson 6 | Where Does True Self-Confidence Come From?

 Complete the following lesson with your child or students to explain how true self-confidence is derived. Figures 6.1 and 6.2 are to be used during the lesson.
Instructor or parent reads:

(Cover Figure 6.1 with a blank sheet of paper. Uncover each line as you discuss it. Uncover and reveal the next step, only after you've asked the questions and allowed your child(ren) time to think and responds.)

What's the difference between true self-confidence and fake self-confidence?

(They can make guesses, but reserve your comments and move to the next question.)

How does a person get self-confidence? Can I give to you? Can you give confidence to someone?

(After they guess, uncover the first line to reveal that true self-confidence is a belief in one's abilities.)

In order to cultivate true self-confidence, we must first understand what true self-confidence really is. Understanding how confidence is derived is necessary if we want to learn how to get it. So, let's break it down.

(Reveal one point at a time and conceal everything below. Together, read and discuss.)

Figure 6.1   Where Confidence Comes From

Self-Confidence is the belief in your abilities. When people are confident, you can see it in their faces and hear it when they talk.	Think about someone who is a confident athlete, musician, artist, reader, student, or whatever. Where does the belief in their abilities come from?
⬇	Why do they believe in their abilities? Isn't it because they have developed skills and they are prepared? Think about the confident people you have in mind. Are they skilled?
Skills and Preparation	So, how did they develop their skills and become prepared?
⬇	They developed their skills from practice. Did they practice once? No, they practiced over and over until their muscles and brains were conditioned.
Practice and Conditioning	So, what made them practice and keep practicing?
⬇	Because they made decisions and choices to practice. Not only that, they took action!
Make Decisions and Choices and Take Action	Why did they decide to practice and keep practicing even though they wanted to do something else?
⬇	Because they were determined. Did you know that determination can grow from successes OR failures we experience? How might success and failure motivate you?
Motivation and Determination	Where did their determination come from? What motivated them to take action?
⬇	They were motivated to take action because of their desire to get something. And that something they wanted was a goal.
Goal	

By understanding how confidence is derived, we can see how confidence is born from a series of events that begins with a goal. More clearly, we can see how one person cannot give another person confidence. Rather, to achieve self-confidence a person *must* go through a series of events (planned or unplanned) in order to grow confidence within. So now that you can see how achieving confidence and academic success starts with setting a goal, let's visualize how we can set goals to achieve more confidence in our lives.

(Reveal one point at a time and conceal everything below. Together, read and discuss.)

Figure 6.2   Setting Goals in Ways that Increase Self-Confidence

Make a Goal
We can create a goal by identifying what we want.
Figure out your goal by asking yourself, "What do I want to happen?"

⬇

Develop Motivation and Enthusiasm
We develop motivation and enthusiasm by identifying why we want to achieve our goal.
Make a list of the reasons you want to achieve your goal.
What do you want life to be like? How do you want to look and feel?
Review this list to fuel your burning desire to achieve your goals.

⬇

Make Good Decisions and Choices
We can make good decisions and choices if we identify what will get us closer to (and farther from) reaching our goals.
Write a list to help you recognize good and bad decisions and choices in everyday life.

⬇

Take Action and Initiative
We can become go-getters if we identify what actions will get us closer to (and farther from) reaching our goals.
Write a list of things you can do on a daily or weekly basis to help you get closer to reaching your goal. What specific actions will you take?

⬇

Develop Determination
We can become more determined if we reflect on the elation of our past successes AND the pain of our past failures.
Write down successes you want to feel and failures you want to avoid.
Review them to make you more determined to reach your goal.

⬇

Practice and Develop Skills
We can gain skills by studying, learning, trying to understand, and practicing.
Write a list of what you need to study and practice to develop
knowledge, understanding, and skill.
Then practice, practice, practice!

Gain Confidence and Poise
We have true confidence when we believe in our abilities. People will see it in our faces and hear it when we talk.
Think of ways you can keep your skills sharp.

I have to warn you, when you strive to reach your goals, you will have to work harder than your classmates. They will play while you're working hard. And, your efforts will stretch you, maybe even to a point where you think you can't take it anymore. But look at it this way, isn't it true when you exercise, you are making your heart work more intensely? Yet by making your heart work harder, won't it also become stronger and healthier? It is when we challenge our hearts, our bodies, and our minds that we become stronger, healthier, and smarter.

Having a goal without working to achieve it is like a farmer who has done no work but goes outside each day and stares at the ground looking for crops to grow. The farmer must prepare the soil, plant the seeds, provide water, and protect the crops from insects. The same is true if we want to achieve our dreams (Joel Osteen).

So where do we start? We begin by making a plan, because "a goal without a plan is just a wish" (Antoine de Saint-Exupery).

Let's pick one goal you think would be most important to your success right now and make a plan using the Goal Planning Worksheet.

Figure 6.3 Goal Planning Worksheet

What is my goal?	My goal is to
Why do I want to achieve my goal? What is the gasoline that will fuel my burning desire to achieve my goal?	I want to achieve this goal because
What good decisions and choices will get me closer to reaching my goal? What bad decisions and choices will prevent me from reaching my goal?	Good decisions and choices I can make are Bad decisions and choices I will not make are
What actions can I take on a daily basis that will help me come closer to reaching my goal? What damaging activities will prevent me from reaching my goal?	Actions I will take on a daily or weekly basis are Damaging activities that I will limit or not do are
What successes and failures have I experienced that will give me strength to reach my goal?	Successful times and feelings I want more of are Failures that hurt me and I don't ever want to feel again are
What do I need to learn and practice?	Things I need to study, learn, or practice more are

Journal 6 | Positively Reminding Students to Achieve Their Goals

 Instructor or parent journals:

Save your child or students' Goal Planning Worksheet from Lesson 6 Where Does True Confidence Come From. Keep it handy, so you can pull it out in the future to remind them of their goal(s).

Journal the ideas you would like to reinforce. How will you say it? ("Great job doing your homework when I know you'd rather be out with your friends right now. Don't let anyone prevent you from feeling and achieving success." Or "Remember where true confidence comes from? You're doing what you need to get it! I'm so proud of you!")

STEP 7 | **MONITOR GOALS**

SHOW HOW MONITORING GOALS CAN BE MOTIVATING

In our world of drive-thru, cosmetic surgery, and pills that almost immediately satisfy hunger, alter bodies, and cure illness, it's hard to compete with quick fixes. Dear parents and teachers, I'm *not* sorry there are no quick fixes or easy solutions for our children with dyslexia, dysgraphia, ADHD, autism, emotional difficulties, etc. Time will present the blessing of these struggles to us, if it hasn't already. Until then, we have to practice patience. Also, cultivating motivation in our children is hard work, and we have to constantly remind ourselves that our work is an *investment* of time and effort. With time and patience, we will achieve significant results.

So how do you motivate a child struggling to reach what seems right now as an impossible goal? A child can reach an "impossible" goal by making attainable advances in small time frames. Depending on the goal, appropriate time frames for kindergarten students may be one class period or half a day. For a 1st or 2nd grade student it may be one day or one week. For 3rd graders and above one week or every report card is an appropriate time frame, depending on the goal.

Once your child or students set their goals, it is essential for them to assess how they are doing at the time frames you set. They can monitor their progress and, over time, they can see what they have accomplished (or not accomplished). In a nurturing and encouraging environment, either way will be motivating for you both. Think about why many children like video games. They may like the characters, interactions, working out strategies, but they really get excited when they "level up," aka make progress. They keep track and it feels good.

Remember to consistently use the skills you've studied so far. Step 1 Control Your Anger and Disappointment. The holes we make in "the fence" will last forever. Step 2 Practice Using Language That Motivates. Use positive and affirmative language, search for potential, and communicate how weaknesses can become strengths with time and practice. If we are constantly focusing on what's "purple," it will be hard to remember the "blue." Step 3 Ask for Cooperation. Remind them what's in it for them, the importance of doing well in school (education is one of the few things we can have that no one can take away, and it gives us more playtime later), and the importance of self-control (if you can't control yourself, someone else will). Step 4 Start Building Self-Efficacy. Part of the reason why children don't change is because they don't think they can. By explaining that we can't reach a destination in one step, controlling our negativity, respecting their dignity, and looking at mistakes in a positive way are a few ways we can start building self-efficacy. Will you be a "Mrs. Desha" (restorer), a "Mrs. Martin" (maintainer), or a "Mrs. Wooldridge" (preserver)? Step 5 Guide Them to Make Good Choices. Frequently, remind them that life is a series of choices. If we prioritize and put the "big rocks" in first, then everything else will fall into place. Step 6 Set Goals in Ways That Increase Self-Confidence. Remind them that true self-confidence begins with a goal, and motivation comes from figuring out our "burning desire," why we want to achieve our goals. Step 7 Monitor Goals. Goal Sessions helps us identify what we could do better and makes us write down action items that will help us come closer to reaching success. Most importantly, monitoring goals gives us opportunities to discuss how our choices affect our outcomes.

Lesson 7 | Monitoring Academic Goals

 Instructor or parent cam complete the following academic goal session with your child or students to help them set and monitor their goals. You can customize your goal session accordingly. Use Figure 7.1 Academic Goal Session.

Remember to ask the student questions in the most positive manner and record your child or student's response. Decide when would be the best time to sit down with your child or student. You may want to have a session after the student receives each report card. Think ahead of time how you will remain positive throughout the goal session.

Also, you cannot set a goal for someone else, so during every academic goal session the goals must come out of your children's or teens' mouths. So, think ahead of time how you can guide them to respond in a certain way by asking specific questions. How will you get their goals have to come out of their mouths? To be most effective, it has to be their ideas.

Figure 7.1   Academic Goal Session

What are my academic goals?

Why is this important?

What grades did I earn in each subject?

Reading

Writing

Listening

Mathematics

Science

Social Studies

Art

Music

Physical Education

What grades do I want to make in each subject?

What subjects do I need to focus on and what *specifically* do I need to do to achieve my goal in each of those subjects?

How will these goals lead to meaningful improvements?

What leverage or reward system can I have to insure that I meet my goal?

Example

Academic Goal Session for a 3rd Grader

What are my academic goals?
(e.g. to get all A's and B's on my report card by the end of the school year)

Why is this important?
(e.g. to feel success, have more choices, play more later in life)

What grades do I want to make in each subject?
(e.g. to earn an A or B in each subject)

What subjects do I need to focus on and what specifically do I need to do to achieve my goal in each of those subjects?
Reading (Work with Mom/tutor so I can improve my reading skills.)
Writing (Work on improving handwriting and spelling.)
Listening/Speaking (Picture what my teacher talks about.)
Mathematics (Practice my addition facts.)
Science (Make flash cards of my science vocabulary.)
Social Studies (Do my homework so I can do better on tests.)
Art (Ask my teacher questions when I don't understand.)
Music (Practice memorizing words to songs at home.)
Physical Education (Use self-discipline during unstructured activities.)

How will these goals lead to meaningful improvements?
(Working on these goals will help me learn how to become a better student. I'm tired of feeling anxious, depressed, stressed out, and overwhelmed. If I learn and improve my skills, the subject will not be so difficult for me. If I become more proficient, then it will take me less time to do my work. I want to feel what it's like to make a good grade and become more confident. I want to learn as much as I can, so I'll be prepared for next year. I want to learn more, so I can have more choices.)

What leverage or reward system can I have to ensure that I meet my goal?
(Mom said she would pay me $5 for every A. She said if I don't make an A, she would give me a hug and love me no matter what.)

Journal 7 | Monitor Goals

 Instructor or parent journals:

When we set goals, we are more likely to see them through if we monitor our progress. Create a chart like the one that follows, Figure 7.2 Monitoring Goals. Fill in some of your child or student's responses from Lesson 7 Academic Goal Sessions. Decide what would be appropriate dates for him or her to monitor their progress (i.e. beginning, middle, and end of year or every grading period). We will study progress monitoring in more detail in future steps.

Note: The following chart could be used to monitor any type of goal whether it's academic, personal, financial, behavioral, musical, fitness, artistic, etc.

Figure 7.2 Monitoring Goals

Subject	Goal	What specific actions can I take to reach my goal?	Checkpoint 1 Date: _____ How am I doing? What else can I do?	Checkpoint 2 Date: _____ How am I doing? Is there anything I should do differently?	Checkpoint 3 Date: _____ What decisions, choices, and actions can I take?

STEP 8 | **BUILD SELF-ESTEEM**

IDENTIFY POOR SELF-ESTEEM

Self-esteem is more than how a person feels about himself or herself. Based on how the person feels, he or she will form a positive or negative attitude and opinion of him or herself. Most people's view of themselves fluctuates somewhat. However, self-esteem can be a problem for children who struggle in school or at home.

When children, teens, or adults' poor self-esteem are not healthily addressed, it can lead to depression, anxiety, and/or aggression towards others.

Feeling isolation, despair, loneliness, void, emptiness, ugly, not needed, a burden, never good enough, wondering, *if I were gone would anyone miss me?*

I want to address these emotions and offer relevant suggestions on how we can help someone with depression or having thoughts of suicide, whether it's your child, a student, friend, or yourself. The following information is not intended replace expert assistance or counseling. If you or someone you know is depressed or having thoughts of suicide, the services of a competent professional should be sought.

EVALUATE, NOT JUDGE

The first thing every person can do is stop judging. We must refrain from passing judgments. We do not know what people have experienced in their life or what they may be currently going through...even our child, family member, or friend we think we know so well, even the people who look like they have it all – the "*successful*" student or the "*beautiful*" girl or boy. Nor should we judge the "*rude bully*" who appears to not have feelings, or the "*idiot*" who does things we think are "*stupid.*"

We must refrain from judging, because there is a cost. The cost of our judgmental words and actions cause inflictions that result in feelings of ugliness, unworthiness, disgust, and self-loathing. Some respond outwardly and create drama in classrooms, homes, marriages, etc. However, most teens and adults learn to keep their emotions inside and private. Over time, they hold on to memories of comments and actions that accumulate and create insecurity, depression, aggression, and/or anxiety. More negative experiences and words can lead to lower self-esteem. When they have low opinions of themselves, they feel they have little worth. They feel rejected or neglected. Their insecurity, depression, aggression, or anxiety can deepen to a dismal point. This is the cost. Passing judgment costs lives.

You may be thinking, "Hold on, how can I prevent myself from judging the *bully* or an *annoying* student, classmate, or coworker who's so *full of himself or herself*? After all, they deserve to be put in their places, don't they? Shouldn't I teach them a lesson?"

If our intent is to truly teach someone a lesson, then we need to find better ways to communicate our lessons. Why? Because, we don't know the cost. As teachers, parents, and coaches, it is not our job to judge them. Instead, let's teach them lessons that inspire, educate, and get them involved. When everyday people reach out, we can turn things around for children, teens, and adults.

BE STRICT, GET UPSET, BUT TELL THEM YOU CARE

Parents, teachers, and coaches, I'm not saying that we have to always be nice. No, we can be strict and firm. And when they do something wrong, consequences must be served. But tell them it's because you care. Ask them, "If I let you get your way, would I be a good parent/teacher/coach?" Explain, "It would be easier if I didn't have this rule or consequence. But I'm standing firm, because I care about you."

We don't always have to be nice to spouses, friends, and family members either. If we don't like something they did, we don't have to agree with them and sing "Kumbaya." We can assess the situation and evaluate what they said or did. Then, we can draw conclusions that help us make healthy decisions. We can be firm about our beliefs, but we do not pass judgments on others. Evaluating, without passing judgments, shows that you care and does not corrode a person's self-esteem.

UNDERSTAND HOW EXPERIENCES, SELF-ESTEEM, AND RESILIENCY ARE RELATED

We think because spouses and family members are close to us, we can say whatever we feel, and they'll get over it. If you spontaneously say whatever you want to your spouse, your marriage will commit suicide. Friendships and family ties can commit suicide too.

By the way, divorces and family feuds are situations that involve our children. They will experience emotional responses, evaluate what happened and what was said. They will draw conclusions, not only about the people involved, but also about themselves, which could affect their self-esteem.

Figure 8.1   The Path to Self-Esteem and Resiliency

Situation	Emotional or Physical Response	Person Evaluates What Happened or What Was Said	Person Draws a Conclusion about the Situation, Themselves, and Others	Person Is Resilient and Self-Esteem Is Intact or Not

How is it that some people can experience trauma, such as a divorce, and bounce back and keep their self-esteem intact? Before we can answer that question, think back to when something traumatic happened to you. What helped you bounce back?

Most likely, someone encouraged you in one of the following ways. Consider how you can do the same for someone else.

1) When a **situation** occurs, a person may need our help translating what happened, so they can understand it more accurately.

For instance, a child may need to hear that their parent's divorce did not happen because of them. It was about their father and mother. Sometimes, all we may need to say is, "It's not about you. It's about them, something they are experiencing."

Or if the situation involved vicious words or actions, we could explain that most likely it was because:

- The person is in physical or emotional pain.
- Something bad happened to them or to someone very close to them.
- They had an expectation and it didn't happen, so they are disappointed, disillusioned, wounded, or jealous.

2) We can also help with their **emotional or physical response** to the situation.

When a child or teen is faced with a situation like bullying or academic failure, it triggers emotional responses. They become conditioned to think, say, and do certain things when they repeatedly find themselves in the same situation over and over again. Some conditioned responses might be to lash out with their words or bodies. For instance, a child who is repeatedly bullied or failing may hurt themselves or others.

Anyone can learn to re-pattern an emotional or physical response that might be damaging. In order to do that, we can teach others (and ourselves) to halt the unhealthy reaction and replace it with a healthy one.

Sometimes our children and students may lash out as us "for no reason." We can help, first and foremost, by keeping our own feelings in check. Many times parents, teachers, and coaches can help a student most by cutting off that unhealthy thing we are about to think, say, or do and replace it with finding one thing that's positive about them.

And, if we're experiencing a negative thought about ourselves, we can replace the unhealthy thought by thinking of three positive things about ourselves. Why three? Because, that's the amount it takes for our self-critical brains to refocus and transition into a positive attitude. Try it the next time you are faced with a situation, and call yourself stupid, ugly, or unloved; stop, and replace that thought with three positive things about yourself.

If we practice this strategy every time, we can condition our brains to break free from negative thought patterns. Over time, we can re-pattern our emotional and physical responses to become more positive. We can do this for ourselves and teach it to others.

3) We could help others **evaluate what happened or what was said** by guiding them to see the lessons or blessings of painful situations. Even in everyday life, we can assess and point out the lessons or blessings in small failures and misfortunes. Here's an example.

My daughter and I had waited until the last minute to shop for her homecoming dress. We went into a few stores and found absolutely nothing and were stressed out. I was kicking myself for waiting until the day of the dance. She was disappointed that nothing looked right, and it was chipping at her self-esteem. I asked myself, "What could be the lesson or blessing in this painful experience?" Of course, the lesson was to not wait until the last moment and not let other things come before my daughter. I apologized to her for my procrastination. The blessing was that my daughter apologized back, saying it was just as much her fault. She bounced back with her self-esteem intact. This experience was not about a dress; it was about experiencing failure and emotions, evaluating the situation, and learning lessons from our painful experience. Cultivating resiliency in everyday life can restore self-esteem and help our children and students tackle life's bigger challenges.

4) We can also help them to stop warping reality and **drawing** false **conclusions**. All too often, people warp how they view themselves. Some of the most *beautiful* people think they are *fat, ugly, awkward,* etc. *Smart* people think they are *dumb*. We must share with them the real definitions of words such as these.

Back to the question: How is it that some people can experience traumas and bounce back and keep their self-esteem intact? Do you see how the four areas above can cultivate self-esteem and resiliency? Read on for more.

DON'T ASSUME

As parents, teachers, coaches, or friends, we can't assume just because someone is *funny*, *successful*, *beautiful*, or *shy* that they are not feeling a void or despair. Or just because someone is frequently *rude* or *full of themselves*, it doesn't mean they are immune from feeling isolation or trauma. How do you know if someone has or is secretly abusing them? Or that someone in their family has been battling cancer or an addiction? Or battling each other, going through a divorce? We do not know what happened to them years ago, yesterday, or today. We must stop assuming. Sometimes there's more to their story, beyond what we see.

RESTORE AND PRESERVE THE SELF-ESTEEM OF TEENAGE CHILDREN

We should not assume that it's normal for teens to withdraw or become rebellious. People with poor self-esteem rely on positive experiences to counteract their negative feelings about themselves. This can be especially true for our teenage children. The following are examples of positive experiences that restore and preserve the self-esteem of teenage children and students.

We can help teens develop a close relationship with adults, peers, and family in the following ways:

- Do things together. Spend large chunks of time together. The only way teens will open up and start sharing is if we make ourselves available.
- Spend time doing their hobbies or interests with them.
- Work together as a family (or class or team) to help them overcome the urge to hurt themselves.
- Make sure they are not alone. Isolation makes it worse. They need to be involved and in a positive environment, not in isolation. Texting and communicating to friends on a computer do not count.
- Set up chores or responsibilities. Have them participate with the family (or class or team) and stay involved. They will whine. They may be sarcastic, but know they will benefit. Even if we feel like we're not making a difference, we will.

Teach teens goal setting:

- Help them create checklists of responsibilities, goals, consequences, and rewards for altered behaviors.
- Provide them with immediate rewards for altered behaviors.
- Involve them in activities (they are interested in) to create ownership and to prevent disenfranchisement.

Develop within teens a sense that they are worthwhile in the following ways:

- Provide them with opportunities to shine.
- Give appropriate attention and affection. Oftentimes, we think our teen children no longer need our hugs. In most cases, touch is missing, and they need it.

SPEAK AUTHENTICALLY

Sometimes we borrow wording from TV, movies, and other people. In this way we've all been handed "scripts" we think we need to follow.

Analyze what you think, say, and do. Sometimes, isn't it tempting to say something sarcastic? Do some words just automatically come out? If so, I want you to change your thinking and I challenge you to speak genuinely. Scripts lie. True feelings that are said with humility do not lie. The more we stick to scripts, the less life we will live. When we dump the scripts and abandon verbal and body reflexes, we will speak from the heart, have more genuine conversations, and experience more fulfilling relationships with our children, spouses, family, and friends.

At times teachers and parents must communicate with teens that may be angry, aggressive, or withdrawn. We tend to avoid them, or we'll mirror their behaviors. We follow scripts and say things that are shamefully sarcastic to appear quick-witted and in control. It is easy to lose our patience and it's almost impossible to feel sorry for them. It can be irresistible to wield our power and teach them a lesson in front of their peers or siblings.

However, we need to remember the reasons why people can behave so poorly. If we try to understand, we can use this insight to help us maintain our composure in the classroom or at home. I can't express how important it is that we not belittle children and teens. Be firm, be strict, serve consequences, but do not take away their dignity. For if we do, what is the cost?

I beg you to consider tossing the scripts and speak from the heart. Set aside your ego and practice having more genuine conversations. You both may feel uncomfortable at first. Be brief. Don't belabor points or preach to them. Instead, tell them what they've done to hurt your feelings. Tell them you're mad or sad *because* you care.

FIND THE ROOT CAUSES AND ADDRESS THEM

A Band-Aid doesn't last a lifetime and neither does a "Band-Aid fix" for a problem. Providing and receiving compliments and positive experiences are not enough. We must study what is causing the insecurity, depression, aggression, and/or anxiety. It would be impossible for me to write everything I would like to say. Do not hesitate to turn to professionals, books, counselors, tutors, and therapists for additional help.

The root causes of difficulties may seem vague and indefinite. Some people do not know where to start or they may be giving credit to an erroneous source. An accurate way to scrutinize root causes is by filling in the blanks of this statement. Pretend you are the child or teen. How would they fill in these blanks?

I am _____ when _____. I feel worse before/during/after _____.

What you initially come up with may be very general, such as:

depressed	I remember and think about...	the holidays
anxious	I think about...	someone comments...
frustrated	I am in school	reading
angry	I am in pain	lifting and carrying

Next, try filling in the blanks one more time with more specific information to dig deeper.

When we become more aware of what, where, and when we are suffering, we can take steps to overcome our challenges. Figure out when self-esteem is lowest. Is it due to an academic, behavioral, social, or emotional challenge? When is it worst?

Reading, journaling, and counseling are excellent ways we can increase our awareness. For example, Eckhart Tolle (1999) shares in his book, *The Power of Now*, how people who experience depression are constantly reliving events of the past. And, those who experience anxiety are worrying excessively about the future. He explains how important it is for us to be conscious of when we drift to the past or future. Reading his book can heighten our awareness and make us more alert, so when we find ourselves obsessively worrying about another time, we can more adequately bring our focus back to the present and what's positive right now.

Enlist help from books, clubs, trainers, apps, events, counselors, tutors, and therapists, and address the root sources. Does something come to mind right now? Make it happen.

BE PRESENT, STAY INVOLVED

Monitor their behaviors; look for anything unusual. Have you noticed any trends? For example, many people suffer from depression during the holidays or in the winter (seasonal affective disorder). Most people don't realize that moods can drop along with the barometric pressure, as well.

When people fall into depression, they are tired and lack the motivation to do things that can counteract depression, such as exercising, cooking healthy foods, getting outside, and making plans with friends and family.

Keep asking them to do things. Invitations count. Don't stop inviting them, even if they say no. It will help them feel included and not feel so isolated.

Do random acts of kindness, like leaving them a note in their lunch, wallet, or doorstep to find later.

Make sure they are eating healthy foods. Parents can wash and cut up vegetables and fruits and place them in clear containers at eyelevel in the refrigerator.

Monitor their activity and make sure they are getting exercise. Blood circulation helps rid the body of toxins, feeds the cells oxygen, and produces hormones that accomplish numerous biochemical processes.

WRITE A LETTER

If you, yourself, are suffering from depression or anxiety, write yourself a letter on a good day when you're feeling positive. Your letter can be handwritten or typed in your phone.

When depression hits, you will be convinced you are alone. So, make certain to exclaim in your letter that you are not alone. Write down who needs you in this world. Think about why each person needs you to live and write it. Tell yourself you really do want to live and to not believe the lies you're thinking. Depression and anxiety are evil liars that skew the truth. Keep your letter with you, to remind you of what is true.

FORGIVE

Perhaps one of the greatest things we can do for our emotional well-being is to forgive others. Step 1 of this book tells the story of monkeys, coconuts, and forgiveness. Take the time to reread it and note how it illustrates the importance of forgiving.

Is there something you need to forgive yourself for? Sometimes we are so unforgiving of ourselves; we beat ourselves up for things we simply cannot undo or change. We should forgive others. It is the right thing to do. And for the same reason, we need to forgive ourselves and accept who we are, what we've done and not done. Just as we can be caring and loving to someone we love, we must be kind and caring to ourselves when we are not perfect. No one is perfect. No one.

If you have a loved one who is depressed, anxious, or has attempted suicide, stop asking, "What if..." Stop thinking, "If only..." Let go.

Stop telling yourself that it's your or someone else's fault. Forgive. It's not any one person's fault. It's way more complicated than that. You have to know this. Trust.

You can get through this. Have faith. From this point forward, do the best you can, move forward, and help others. Don't miss out on life. Make the most of what you have right now.

Lesson 8 | The $10 Bill

 For this activity you will need a $10 bill. Complete the following lesson with your child or a classroom of students to send a more permanent message regarding their self-worth.
Instructor or parent reads:

Hold up a crisp $10 dollar bill. Hold it for everyone to see.

Do you want this $10 dollar bill? (Surely, everyone will say yes)

Crumple the bill.

Do you still want it?

Rip a small tear on top of the bill and ask again.

Do you still want this bill?

Drop it to the ground and stomp on it.

Now that I have crumpled this bill, frayed it, and stomped on it do you still want it? (Yes)

Why? Why do you still want it? (The answer you're looking for is because it's still worth $10 dollars.)

Did you know that each one of you is just like this $10 bill? Know that people may stomp on you, crumple you with their mean words, rip into you, and do all kinds of mean things to you. Bad things happen to us all, it's happened to me, it will happen to you, but remember... no one can ever take away what you're worth. Just because someone may crumple you with their mean words, they cannot reduce how much you're worth. And I tell you now, you're worth way more than this $10 bill. Always remember that.

Give the $10 bill to the person.

Keep this $10 bill as a reminder. If you want to spend it, take a photo of it and keep the photo as a reminder that no one can take away what you're worth.

Journal 8 | Make Them Feel Like a Million Bucks

 Instructor or parent journals:

Think of ways you are hurting your child, student, or someone you love. What mean words make them crumple? What speech rips them in half? What actions stomp out their joy? What can you do instead?

How are others hurting your child or students? What can you do about it?

The University of Texas Counseling and Mental Health Center (2015) suggests the following childhood experiences can contribute to healthy self-esteem:

- Being listened to
- Being spoken to respectfully
- Getting appropriate attention and affection
- Having accomplishments recognized and mistakes or failures acknowledged and accepted

Which of the activities in the list above are you doing? Refer to the list to help you generate ideas of things you can do and say on a daily basis.

STEP 9 | **ADDRESS SELF-DISCIPLINE**

EXPLAIN WHY SELF-DISCIPLINE IS IMPORTANT

Why is self-discipline important? What does it mean to be self-disciplined? When we are self-disciplined, we can look beyond what we'd rather be doing and do what needs to be done instead. This isn't always easy. However, if we can imagine how our lives would be better and easier later, then the task of sacrificing something we want (to do) now could help us develop self-discipline. Famous author, Stephen Covey, pointed out how "sacrifice is giving up something—even something good—for something better" (Covey, 2004, 166). He also said, "Only the disciplined are truly free. The undisciplined are slaves to moods, appetites and passions" (Covey, 74).

However, there are times when adults, teens, and children will not be motivated by simply knowing this positive message. Sometimes, it's a negative experience that spurs us to take action. Here are two stories about how parents used negative experiences to motivate their children.

The Northwest Corner

A long time ago I was listening to a radio show on NPR. The guest speaker was telling us about her trials with school and how her dad had inspired her. I do wish I had written down the name of the woman, so I could give her proper credit. And I hope that I do her justice by remembering correctly the details of her story that I heard so long ago.

The speaker began by telling us listeners how she and her sister had been struggling in school. Her dad sat them down to say that he'd gotten their last report cards and he told them flatly that the poor grades they have been receiving were no longer acceptable. She, being the older sister, spoke up, by saying, "Our grades aren't *that* bad." He responded, "So you're satisfied with making these grades?" She returned, "Yes, I'm satisfied." To that he said, "Alrighty then, set your alarms for 5:30 in the morn, we're going on a trip."

Sure enough, at 5:30 they woke to the alarm and the smell of breakfast. Her dad told them, "Eat hearty, you'll be needin' it today." After breakfast they hopped into the truck and their dad drove them out to the northwest corner of their property. He said, "You see all these rocks all over. Y'all got 'til 2:00 to move 'em all to this spot." The girls were stunned as they watched their dad leave. By 12:00 they were exhausted, and her younger sister was crying. By 2:00 the rocks had all been moved and their dad came back to pick them up. The oldest daughter cried, "Dad why did you do that? Why did you make us do all that hard work?" He replied, "You said you were satisfied with your grades. So, I figured I needed to prepare y'all for the work y'all have ahead of ya'. It's my job to prepare you for the future an' if this is the kind of work y'all want to do, then it's better you work up to it. Come 18, I don't want you to be shocked at what all you got to do."

I listened intently as the speaker shared with us how that day changed her and her sister's lives. Her dad was brilliant. He didn't have to raise his voice, nor was he forcing them to make good grades. Rather he communicated meaning and purpose to his daughters *in his own way*, in a way that inspired change and stayed with them all their lives.

I'm not telling you to take your kids to the northwest corner of your property. My point is this, as parents we hate to see our children suffer, but sometimes it has to be the negative that spurs them into action. And when the sting is gone, a seed will have been planted, a seed, which will produce a more fruitful mentality.

Erin Brockovich

At times I read stories to my students from the book, *Great Failures of the Extremely Successful: Mistakes, Adversity, Failure and Other Steppingstones to Success*. The author, Steve Young, shares the following about one of my heroes, Erin Brockovich.

Erin Brockovich fought for the residents of Hinkley, California who had been poisoned by chromium VI. At the time, it was the biggest lawsuit settled in U.S. History. What you may not know is that Erin Brockovich is dyslexic and had struggled in school. She says that her mom and dad were her inspiration. The following is a letter Erin's mom wrote to her.

"In view of your latest report card, your parents have decided the following course of action is necessary. You will have no personal phone use. Your grades can be no less than a "C." You may not partake in after-school activities. Television will be limited. We are not happy having to restrict your social life, but you have to cut out time-wasting habits. You haven't been able to discipline yourself or adhere to proper study habits. You must have self-discipline and self-determination. You have wonderful natural abilities. Face up to the fact that you and no one else can put in the time. Don't pass on the blame. Apply yourself each day to the task at hand. Try to not be easily distracted by monkey business. Don't worry about popularity. You're fortunate to have friends and you will still have them. Give schoolwork a good hard try and you will be surprised at what you learn. Stick-to-itiveness is important. You have to develop the habit of perseverance. Take this with the right attitude. We love you and care about your development. Use all your potential to grow into a mature person. We love you and who you are, but we need assurance that you're doing your best, and it is our responsibility to see that you do it" (Young, 2002, 4).

COUNTER NEGATIVITY WITH CARE

The mother and father in the previous two stories are examples of parents who used a negative circumstance to increase their children's awareness of self-discipline and spurred their children into action. They both communicated meaning and purpose in their own loving, positive, strict way! They countered what could be perceived as negative and harsh by also telling their children they are being "mean" because they love them.

Children need to hear from their parents or teachers, "If I let you off the hook, would I be doing you a favor? Is that love? I'm being 'mean' because I care about you today, a year from now and 10 years from now."

Lesson 9 | The Unwritten Law of Parenthood

Complete the following lesson with your child or students when you absolutely must have their cooperation. Teachers, can use the version below.
Parent reads:

The "Unwritten Law of Parenthood" has just gone into effect! Let me tell you what that means.

First, imagine that you have children. You're the parent. And every time you ask your children to do something they don't listen to you. You wouldn't stand for it, would you? (Allow for a productive pause.)

You know why?

Because of the Unwritten Law of Parenthood = I had to do what my parents told me to do. It's my turn to tell my children what to do. And when you're a parent, you will tell your children what to do. (Productive Pause)

Tell me this - would it be fair if my parents told me what to do and now my children tell me what to do? You wouldn't stand for that, and *neither will I.*

Instructor reads privately to a student:

Imagine that you're a teacher. You have your own classroom and students. And every time you ask your students to do something, they don't listen to you. It would be completely frustrating, wouldn't it? How would you be able to teach them what they need to know before the end of the school year? You wouldn't stand for it, would you? (Allow for a productive pause.)

Think of it this way, I had to do what my teacher told me to do. It's my turn to tell my students what to do so they will learn. And if or when you're a teacher, you will tell your students what to do. (Productive Pause)

Tell me this - would it be fair if my teachers had told me what to do all these years and now that I'm a teacher, my students tell me what to do? You wouldn't stand for that, and *neither will I.*

Journal 9 | Self-Discipline Plan

 Instructor or parent journals:

Reread your journal entries for Journal 1 Kick-Start Respect and Journal 4 Kick-Start Self-Efficacy. Do you have additional comments you would like to add? Create a self-discipline plan based on the people and circumstances you wrote about or create a plan for someone new.

STEP 10 | ADDRESS PATTERNS OF INAPPROPRIATE BEHAVIOR

DON'T TAKE IT PERSONAL

If you're seeing a pattern of undesirable behaviors from your child or students, don't take it personally. Instead, try to understand the root causes of their poor behavioral choices. This way, you will be more likely to remain calm and to address problem behaviors. This step is intended to help create awareness and offer strategies that will engage your most challenging children. You'll receive more intensive instruction in future steps.

DEFINE THE BEHAVIOR

Define the problem behavior. What does it look, sound, or feel like? Write down specifically what your child or teen is thinking, saying, and doing that is problematic. Decide if your goal is to reduce or eliminate an unwanted behavior or to increase a desired behavior.

FIND OUT WHAT FUNCTION THE BEHAVIOR SERVES

Behaviors serve a function. It may be to get something (attention, good grades, praise, something tangible). Or, it may be to avoid or escape from something (failure, punishment, embarrassment). Or, it could be because they need to satisfy sensory needs (twirl hair, touch walls, hum, play with pencil).

Start jotting down notes to find out which function(s) the behavior serves. To find the function, ask yourself, "Is this child trying to get something? Or to avoid something? Or to satisfy sensory needs?"

Example

6th grade student frequently comes to Math class without a pencil. The teacher wants to stop loaning him pencils because he "accidentally" breaks them. On days he doesn't snap them in half, the lead breaks and he gets up multiple times to sharpen his pencil.

To find the function, the teacher moved the student to a spot that was convenient to observe him and jot notes. His notes revealed that the student would snap his pencils and break the lead to avoid doing his classwork.

FIND THE REASONS FOR THE MISBEHAVIOR

Finding the reason why someone does something gives a parent or teacher more information. Rudolf Dreikurs and Alfred Adler are two psychologists from the early 1900's. They insightfully describe the four "Mistaken Goals" behind children's misbehaviors. According to them, there are four reasons children misbehave:

- Attention
- Power
- Revenge
- Avoidance of Failure

If you are not familiar with the four "Mistaken Goals" of misbehavior, take 5 minutes to search the Internet and print out one of the many charts available for free. Refer to it in your observations.

Example

To find the reasons for the student's misbehavior, the teacher asked him if he would like to have lunch in his classroom. The student said no but showed up anyway. The teacher asked a few questions to get to know his student. Seen any movies lately? What elementary school did you go to? What was your favorite thing there? Least favorite? The student shared how he hated his Math class.

After their lunch and more observations, the teacher began to realize the student was not seeking attention, power, or revenge. He was avoiding failing. He wasn't failing; his pencil was.

FIGURE OUT POSSIBLE ANTECEDENTS

Next, try to figure out what happens before the inappropriate behavior. The following are a few things to consider:

- Does the student understand what you're saying/asking?
- Is the student having difficulty processing directions?
- Check to see who is near the student? Proximity to others may be a problem?
- Do transitions to different places or activities seem to cause stress/anxiety/silliness?
- What might be frustrating the child or teen?

- Do you see signs of uninterested and bored behavior?
- Is the child or teen about to fail?
- What could be sources of distractions?
- Is the child tactile? Does he or she need to touch textures, items, or others often?

Example

The teacher began to notice that the student's pencil malfunctions would happen while he was working on math problems involving multiplication and division. The teacher went back to his student's assessments and noticed he scored very low in computational fluency. No wonder, his student's lack of basic skills made him feel like a failure and miserable.

PRACTICE USING DIFFERENT STRATEGIES AND MONITOR PROGRESS

Once we've defined the child or teen's behavior, thought about what function the behavior serves, and considered the reasons for the behavior and possible antecedents, then we can experiment with different strategies to achieve results.

I can't stress the importance of monitoring our child or challenging students' progress. Here's how. First, jot down notes and track the frequency of the person's behaviors. Next, choose one of the following strategies you think will make the most difference. Try using the strategy a few times and document the results each time. If it does not improve the child's behavior, try another strategy and record what happens.

Here are a few strategies you may want to try. Remember to record how they respond.

Differentiate Instruction and/or Materials

Most teachers and parents understand that all children are not alike. Ironically, many teachers find it extremely difficult to treat children in a classroom differently. Likewise, parents with multiple children may feel the same. However, one of the most powerful things we can do cultivate academic, behavioral, and emotional success is to honor their differences. It is so important, that a future step is devoted to it.

We can experiment with changing how we parent and teach and then notice the differences in a children's output. We can also differentiate our activities, curriculum, materials, and interventions in an effort to honor our students' differences.

Reteach Fundamental Skills

A teacher or parent can customize their instruction, materials, and approach to fill gaps in academic knowledge and skills.

Example

The 6th grade teacher recruited parent volunteers to tutor a couple of students. Volunteers were able to meet with individual students every morning for 15 minutes before school started. The teacher gave the parent volunteer flash cards for addition the first week, subtraction the second, multiplication the third, and division the fourth week. The following month, the teacher observed that both students asked to get water and go to the bathroom less often. Plus, they had fewer missing assignments, showed less frustration, and had fewer outbursts (and broken pencils).

Change How You Speak to or Treat a Child

Sometimes switching something we say or how we treat a child can stimulate change. No matter how we feel about certain children or teens, when they are angry, we should ask them, "Are you okay? Are you hurt?" Let them know, "First and foremost your safety and well-being are important to me." Then, ask what happened from the beginning. Really listen and try to understand their perspectives, even if you feel they are at fault. Depending on what they say, we can ask questions to help them reflect on (1) what could have triggered the incident, (2) what may have escalated it, (3) what choices/ decisions/words/actions did they take and what could have been better, (4) some possible solutions, and (5) appropriate consequences or resolutions. If a student has an IEP or 504 Accommodations, follow the guidelines.

We should prepare a plan for how we could prevent an escalation of events in our classrooms (ahead of time) with administrators or counselors. For example, we could send a student who is getting worked up to a designated staff member for a brief, friendly visit. We can simply say to the student, "You are not in trouble. I am concerned and would like for you to see the counselor for a short visit." The counselor could be a sounding board and explain to the student that sometimes people need to get their feelings out. If the student doesn't want to talk, then the counselor could say, "If you need anything, I'm here for you," and send them back to class. The student may still be upset, but we will have prevented an escalation affecting everyone in the classroom.

Example

After achieving success with "the pencil breaker," the 6th grade teacher decided to change the way she would handle another challenging and more aggressive student. When she noticed his behavior beginning to escalate, she called him to her desk and she privately asked him if he was okay. The student said he was fine. She quietly responded, "Well if you need to talk, I'm here." The next day, she noticed he was becoming agitated and so she called him over and asked again. This time, his face became red and his eyes watered.

He told her his parents had been fighting, and he felt like he was in the middle. She listened and repeated that he can always talk to her. After tracking his aggressiveness for a month, she was heartened to see how dramatically his number of outbursts had dropped since the day he confided in her.

When A Student Refuses to Work, Ask If They Need Help

When students are not doing their work, we can ask if they need clarification of the directions or if someone is disturbing them. Often, we may only need to restate the directions using different wording or ask if they'd like to get water or go to the nurse. Instructors should document what type of assignment the student is refusing to complete along with the skills required. Keep track and note any patterns. Does the student refuse to work on assignments that correspond to an area of weakness? Document as much as possible to determine if the student would benefit from tutoring (reteaching of fundamental skills), differentiating instruction, or changing how you speak to and treat them?

Use Social Reinforcements and Forms of Praise

Research shows that the positive things "bad" students do in classrooms go unrecognized. However, if complimenting "good" students encourages more "good" behavior, then why do we deny the same encouragement to our "troublemakers?"

Some teachers may be reluctant to recognize or reward the "bad" student. They may think that by acknowledging the student in any way may acknowledge the "bad" things he or she has done. They prefer to have that student serve as an example and reminder to other students that this is what happens when you cannot behave.

We should acknowledge, in a casual manner, positive student behaviors, such as hard work, kindness, and dependability. It is especially important to affirm teens and students who struggle. Keep in mind, every classroom has a few students who are uncomfortable when they receive praise. They still need it, just not publicly. We can communicate our nonchalant praise privately.

We can use our voices, facial expressions, gestures, graphics, and activities to reinforce students making an effort. Here are a variety of things we can do to encourage them to keep it up:

- Immediately give attention involving active listening. Make a point to listen to what they have to say before responding.
- Immediately show interest in a subtle way.
- Privately say or write words of encouragement. Remember, some students may act unfavorably when they receive public compliments or attention.
- Allow them to care for a class pet or take on a new responsibility or leadership role.

- Stand nearby or sit beside them.
- Smile, nod, or give them the thumbs up without others seeing.
- Give them a pat on the back, a high five, or fist bump.
- Give them computer time or free reading or drawing time.
- Send a positive note home to a parent.
- Give them a tic-tac-toe or bingo card and fill in a space with a happy face. When they get a tic-tac-toe or bingo or a blackout, reward them with a "You win!"
- Give the entire class/family a reward and say, "Just because," and then look the child/teen's way.

Remember, some children (especially those with oppositional defiance) may not want attention called to them, not even the good kind. So do not make a production out of it because you may get the opposite reaction from what you would expect. So, try whispering privately to the student good job for ___. Then announce to the class, "Class, something wonderful has just happened and I want to reward you all with 5 minutes extra recess." The student who needs to know will know, and that's what matters most.

Example

A father who worked two jobs was having a hard time getting his 5th grade daughter to complete her homework independently every night. The first night she completed her homework, he drew a smiley face on it. He said, "This is how I feel when you work hard. Keep up the good work!" A couple days later she completed her homework again. He grabbed a piece of paper and drew a dog with a big smile. He said, "Now look what you've done. You made the dog smile too!" The dad hung his dog picture on the refrigerator. A few days later, he replaced it with drawing of a frog leaping for joy. Another night he drew fireworks; another night he drew a sun (wearing sunglasses) beaming and smiling. The following month he observed that he did not have one argument with his daughter about completing her homework.

Prevent Minor Behaviors in the Classroom

- Say hello to each student as they walk into the classroom.
- Have the day's activity and instructions on the board before they walk into the classroom.
- Make certain to pronounce everyone's names correctly and say their names often.
- Have students vote on rules, procedures, and consequences for you and them.
- Reward positive behaviors (e.g. positive notes, brain teasers, riddles, drawing).
- Keep students active, and constantly ask questions throughout class.
- Keep students engaged with less transition time, faster presentation rates, and frequently asking students questions about what they are learning.

Tell Them What's In It for Them

Plan a brief discussion with our children or students to consider the importance of education or the area they need to improve. Tell them what's in it for them.

It might go something like this:

Adult: Don't you just hate being told what to do?
Child: I can't stand it! I can't wait until I'm older.
Adult: You know, people won't stop telling you what to do just because you're an adult. The more education you have, there will be fewer people who will tell you what to do. In life, whoever has the knowledge has the power, more choices, and control over their life.

Figure 10.1   Importance of Education

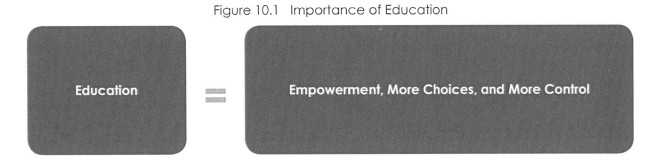

Discuss Facial Expressions and Tone

Some children need more practice with social skills than their classmates. In a discussion, they may be able to tell us the proper thing to do in a certain social situation but fail to do so when placed in that very same situation. A breakdown occurs when they fail to translate social cues such as body language and then do not follow through with the appropriate and expected behavior. Taking the correct action requires forethought and time for the child to think about choosing the appropriate behavior. A parent or teacher can create awareness that triggers forethought. For instance, we can talk about body language (facial expressions and tone), expectations, and appropriate responses.

State the Facts

Sometimes, we can just state plain, simple facts. It might go something like this:

Adult: Tek, we do not hit.
Child: He started it.
Adult: We do not hit, period.
Child: He hit me first.
Adult: I did not see. Hitting back doesn't solve anything, so we do not hit.

Create Signals to Communicate Expected Behaviors

Inappropriate or undesired behaviors can be addressed in a non-blaming and non-punitive way. Rather than always using words (and tone) to tell a student he or she is not behaving properly, we can create hand signals to communicate the expected behavior. Focus on only one or two behaviors at a time. For example, a parent watching her child's attention drift from the Tae Kwon Do instructor can point her index finger to her eye and then to the instructor. Or a teacher can tug on his ear to signal to a student to stop talking and listen. In this way, a parent or teacher can intervene at an appropriate time by simply giving a signal triggering the child to think about what he or she is doing.

Create Verbal Cues

Verbal cues could also be used, whereby one word acts as a signal triggering the child to think about what he or she is doing or needs to do. For a student lacking self-control who cannot stop what he or she is doing to follow your instructions, we could use the following cues.

"One" means *Stop what I am doing.*
"Two" means *Say to myself over and over what I am supposed to be doing until I do it.*
"Three" means *Do it or else* _____ (the consequence).

To be successful, we begin by taking the child aside and discussing the undesired behavior. Together decide on a signal or verbal cue together and consequences that will follow if the agreed signal is ignored. We may also ask younger students to draw a picture of what the signal looks like or to write the word(s) and what they mean.

For impact and a lasting impression, we must use words that *create pictures* in the child's mind. And most importantly, we should give *meaning and purpose* as to *why* he or she must work on correcting the undesired behavior.

TEACH "INVENTION" GOAL SETTING

Some teachers and parents cannot understand why their children couldn't *just do* what they are asking. They also may not think they have the time to "go through the trouble" to modify what they are doing. However, if we make the adjustments, after one month, we will observe how much time, energy, and frustration our efforts save us.

Don't worry if you try one of the techniques and aren't successful. Nor should you fret if one worked at first, but no longer does. The beautiful thing about differentiating instruction is that you can continually modify and change what you do to get results.

Customizing and modifying what you are doing is essential, if you want someone to change habitual or conditioned behaviors. Think about the behaviors (goals) you want to help them improve. Write a list of techniques you could try in order to spark change in their behaviors. Make choices and take action. Then, document the results. Assess how you are doing. Ponder if, and how, their behaviors (goals) and needs have changed. Make new goals and write down what else you could do or not do. Then revise your list of techniques to continue the goal setting cycle.

After you've initiated this process, you're ready to teach your child or students "invention" goal setting in the following lesson. It is a creative way to share insight that will empower them to take control of their bodies, minds, and destiny.

Lesson 10 | Inventing Ourselves by Goal Setting

 Instructor or parent reads to show how we can break old patterns and invent ourselves by goal setting:

Can I get from one side of the room to the other side in one step? (No) Nor can I get from who I am today to the person I want to be in one day or one week. Becoming who we are is a process, much like an inventor creating an invention. Whether we realize it or not, we are in the process of inventing ourselves.

To start this process, I want you to start thinking about the person you would like to become. What does that person look like? Describe what you want to achieve? Picture the person you want to be. How does that person feel? What does that person believe in? What would you like others to say about you?

Imagine you're Thomas Edison who created the light bulb. Before he created a functional light bulb, what did he do? What had to happen before his invention became a reality? Take a few guesses before we read on. Really, try to think about it before we keep going. What did he have to do to create it?

He had to try new and different ideas, didn't he?
Do you think he had to overcome obstacles?
How many times do you think he failed?
It is widely known that thousands of his experiments failed. He kept trying.
His failures made him more determined.
He researched, studied, and asked questions. He found answers and solved problems.
He had a plan. And, he revised it as he learned new information.
He became more aware and prepared.
He made decisions and choices. He took action.
Did he do it all by himself? No, he asked for help and accepted support from others.

Before Edison did all of these things, before he even gathered his materials, what did he have to have? VISION, he had a picture in his mind of what he wanted to accomplish.

In order to invent ourselves, we must do everything Edison did. We can design and build who we are to become - and it **starts with creating a vision**. We don't have to see the complete picture now, but we must start thinking about the person we'd like to become. What does that person look like? What do you want to achieve? Start picturing yourself doing jobs, hobbies, and activities.

After generating ideas, then we can **set goals** based on what we want to achieve. There are different types of goals:

- School, work, career
- Hobbies, interests
- Relationships
- Health, fitness, and well-being
- Faith, religious, spiritual

What would you like to improve? Be specific. What would you like to accomplish? For example, instead of saying, "I want to make better grades," you could say, "I want to improve my grade in Math." Next, think of how you can include measures and timeframes. "I want to make an A in Math by the end of the school year."

Once we have a specific goal that includes a measure and timeframe, we can **create a "grocery list" of to do's** - just like like writing down everything we need from the grocery store. What can happen if we don't write an item on our grocery list? Here's what happens to most of us. We'll go down the aisle that has the item we need, and we'll pass right by it. We may even look right at it! We leave the store, and guess what? When we need it, we won't have it.

Similarly, we should write a "grocery list" of to do's. If we write down what we need to do to accomplish our goals, then we'll be more likely to actually to do them. And when opportunities present themselves in our daily lives, we won't be caught off guard or leave chance or circumstance to take care of our goals. Our focus will be on our to do list, which will **increase our awareness**.

Figure 10.2   (Re)Inventing Yourself Starts with Creating a Vision

Create a vision ⟩ Set goals ⟩ Create a "grocery list" of to do's ⟩ Increase our awareness ⟩

With our increased awareness we will **see opportunities**, **make smarter decisions and choices**, and **take deliberate actions** that will help us reach our goal(s). What decisions and choices can you make that will help you achieve your goals?

Over time, our choices and **sustained focus and effort** will get us closer and closer to making our visions become reality. Decide how you will sustain your focus and effort. How will you stay motivated and focused on your goals?

Figure 10.3   (Re)Inventing Ourselves Requires Awareness

See opportunities ⟩ Make smarter decisions and choices ⟩ Take deliberate actions ⟩ Sustain focus and effort ⟩

Edison continually monitored his progress. Each time his experiments failed he learned more. He thought deeply about what he needed to do differently. He set new goals, read, asked questions, and asked others for help. He became more aware and used his new awareness to make changes and smarter decisions. He took deliberate actions and kept his focus. Regularly, he monitored his success (and failure), decided what to do differently, and set new goals. In this same manner, we can invent ourselves by goal setting.

Figure 10.4   Becoming the Greatest Invention We'll Ever Create

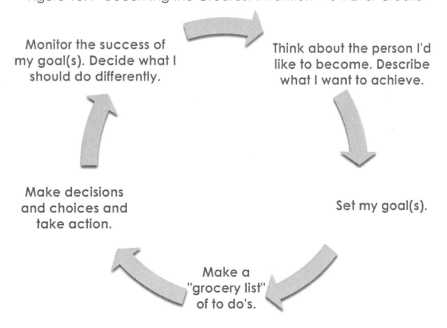

Monitor the success of my goal(s). Decide what I should do differently.

Think about the person I'd like to become. Describe what I want to achieve.

Set my goal(s).

Make a "grocery list" of to do's.

Make decisions and choices and take action.

Journal 10 | Identify Patterns, Triggers, Strategies and Behavior Changes

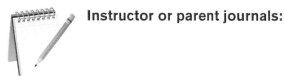 **Instructor or parent journals:**

Write about your student or child's problem behaviors in the classroom or at home. Jot down notes to find out what function each behavior serves (e.g. to get something, avoid or escape from something, sensory). What is the reason(s) for the misbehavior? (e.g. attention, power, revenge, avoidance of failure) Can you identify what triggers (or happens before) the misbehavior? What makes the behavior escalate? What strategies from Step 10 could you use to increase the child's awareness? Draw up a plan of how you will implement some of the strategies. How will you monitor your progress, so you can see what works and doesn't work?

Figure 10.5   Understanding Problem Behaviors and Solutions

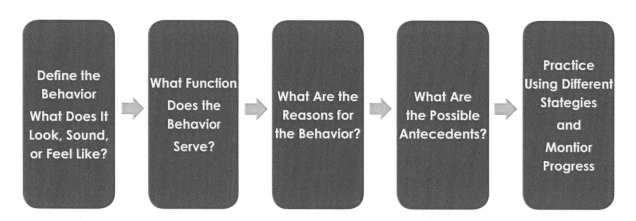

In order for a student to improve or change a behavior, the student must perceive the task is worth doing, plus the student must feel that it is possible to achieve. Reflect and write down who your target student(s) are. What improvements would you like to see? How can you communicate that what you're asking them to do is worth doing? How can you get them to feel it is possible to achieve?

Figure 10.5   Changing Behavior

STEP 11 | **EXPLAIN ACCOUNTABILITY**

EXPLORE REASONS WHY FOLLOWING RULES MAY BE DIFFICULT

Many students have a hard time following rules because they struggle with protocols and multi-step instructions. For example, students with dyslexia have a difficult time memorizing lists of steps. They also struggle with sequencing, so sometimes they do things out of order (e.g. reading, spelling, following instructions). Younger students with ADHD can struggle with impulsivity, so they may say they have strong emotional reasons that prevent them from conjuring the self-discipline.

Nevertheless, just because someone has dyslexia, ADHD, autism, etc., doesn't mean they will always struggle with the challenges associated with their learning differences. Children who are identified with learning disabilities can outperform children who do not have learning disabilities. How? Because when students are identified, parents and instructors can provide interventions that address the root causes of their issues. Also, parents, teachers, tutors, coaches, and counselors have a better understanding of what will help those students become more successful. They are often taught strategies for coping, or they may receive understanding.

On the other hand, many students who have learning disabilities and are not identified, may experience strenuous challenges without understanding why. Their frustration may manifest itself in forms of undesirable classroom behaviors, which often spill over into their home lives. Over time, they may experience depression, anger, vehemence, and/ or rebellion. When following protocols becomes a daily struggle, we should consider the various reasons why.

STRENGTHEN ACCOUNTABILITY

Whether a student has a learning disability or not, bad behavior and broken rules should not be excused. When children fail to achieve progress in their behaviors, teachers and parents should hold their children accountable. By ignoring wrongdoing, some teachers and parents are harming their children and preventing them from success. Turning a blind eye may be the less stressful option, but it's not doing the student a favor.

Children need firm parents, teachers, coaches, and principals to enforce rules, set boundaries, and communicate expectations. However, if accountability is handled in the wrong way, it could make students resentful and therefore increase the very behavior you want to limit! That's why punitive discipline should not be used to control their behavior. Some examples of punitive "discipline" are yelling, threatening, insulting, hitting, spanking, and isolating them from others (e.g. suspension from school, in-school suspension). These acts humiliate children and ostracize them. These tactics may gain you some temporary control of your classroom, home, or school; but prepare yourself for immediate or future retaliation and rebellion.

No doubt, students should be suspended from school for fighting, bringing a weapon to school, drugs, and other major offenses. But lack of respect, clowning around, and not following class rules are not good reasons for taking children out of the classrooms. They will fall further behind, and miss valuable lessons, which creates anxiety, ill feelings, and deficits in their knowledge and skills. These children need education. They need our help. They need us to exercise approaches similar to the ones in this book.

Teachers and parents are the boss. We set the rules and limits. However, we need to do it respectfully and with empathy. By doing so, we can strengthen accountability in a way that will cultivate cooperation and respect.

Think about what the word *accountability* really means. Account-ability means to record and count their abilities (not their inabilities).

We can strengthen a student's account-ability by:

1) Setting standards
2) Measuring (account) their progress (ability)
3) Providing incentive and motivation to achieve
4) During this process, use an it's-not-my-life-it's-yours mentality.

SET STANDARDS

The most basic way you can set standards is by having classroom or house rules. Avoid setting the rules yourself. Cultivate respect and cooperation by asking students to set and vote on rules themselves.

So, if you are a teacher, for example, guide them to come up with rules for you first. Each should be stated as an ability, not an inability. In other words, guide them to tell you what you should do, not what you shouldn't do. Here are a few ideas of rules students can set for teachers.

- Have lessons ready.
- Grade and hand back work weekly.
- Create a positive learning environment.

- Explain tasks and assignments clearly. If students do not understand, explain it in a different way.
- Be available for extra help at scheduled times each day.
- Supply students with materials and activities.
- Speak respectfully.
- Listen.
- Help students be the best they can be.
- Give class rewards.
- Enforce consequences.

Next, have them come up for rules for themselves. Write down the ones you agree on. Elementary school children may need you to discuss the benefits of each rule. You may want them to give examples or ask them to discuss behaviors and consequences.

You may want to ask students to ratify the rules. You can say, "All in favor of making these our rules can do so by raising their hands. By raising our hands, we are agreeing that we understand why these must be put into effect and we will try our best to follow them." Make the commitment complete with handshakes. Give students a copy for parents to sign and return. Everyone should decide on a reward. And don't *ever* threaten to take away a reward that has already been earned.

MEASURE (ACCOUNT) THEIR PROGRESS (ABILITY)

Use some type of visual to record and measure progress. Replace boring progress monitoring charts with visuals you or your children create. For example, a parent can post a bingo board on the refrigerator. Every day the child comes home from school with a positive report, he or she will get to fill in a spot. Younger students may need to see progress sooner. If that's the case, use a tic-tac-toe board. Children and teens that play video games, such as *Minecraft*, *Super Mario*, or *World of Warcraft*, could create their own map for homework. Then, they could use it to record their progress. Over time, they can see how they advance or "level up" and be motivated to work hard to do "the impossible." They could also monitor their progress using a number of visuals, like lacrosse goals, swim laps, golf courses, obstacle courses, amusement parks, etc.

Most importantly, date and collect the progress monitoring visuals over time so you can chart the data. This will motivate and inspire students to make "the impossible" possible.

PROVIDE INCENTIVE TO ACHIEVE

To reward children for their hard work, provide a small, but meaningful incentive each time they make a bingo or a tic-tac-toe. Older children can be rewarded when they blackout their bingo board. It doesn't have to be something of value; it just has to be meaningful.

Also, never take away or threaten to take away anything they've earned! Remember, you're accounting their abilities, not their inabilities.

Collect their bingo boards so they can witness their progress, which can also be motivating. Also, be sure to ask them, "What's the secret to your success?" So they can connect their actions to the outcomes.

MOTIVATE BY EXPLAINING, "I'M MEAN BECAUSE I CARE"

Mention that you are bound by your classroom/family rules, which were voted on. You must enforce them. Explain that holding them accountable shows you care. It's one of the ways you are putting your love/care into action.

ACKNOWLEDGE GOOD BEHAVIORS

Over time, as you acknowledge the good they do, they will be more likely to acknowledge their faults and hold themselves accountable.

REMIND THEM, "IT'S NOT MY LIFE, IT'S YOURS."

When children misbehave, remind them you're not the one who misbehaved, they did. You didn't decide to talk during instructional time, they did. This communicates that breaking a rule is a choice. Therefore, the consequence is something they decided, not you.

Say, "When you (<u>behavior</u>), you are electing to (<u>consequence</u>)."

Say, "When you say no/yes to (<u>behavior</u>), you are saying no/yes to (<u>consequence</u>)."

Follow up with Lesson 11 The Painting.

Lesson 11 | The Painting

For this activity you will need a painting with heavy brushstrokes. Complete the following lesson with your child or students to convey that *the person we are really accountable to is our self.*. Show the painting and point out how the artist uses heavy brushstrokes.
Instructor or parent reads:

Each one of us is responsible for making a painting out of our lives. And just as all artists plan their masterpieces before they make them— whether you know it or not—right now you are planning how your life will be, by the choices you make each and every day. Every day you choose the colors and the brushstrokes that will make the painting of your life.

In the end, the choices that you make, and the effort you put into it, will be reflected in your painting. And the choices you make will also dictate whether you will look upon your painting with pride or with regret.

I've made my painting and I cannot make yours for you. It is up to you to use foresight and make conscious decisions each and every day to make your painting real.

Lesson 11 continued I Private Discussion on an As Needed Basis

Privately discuss the following with your child or student when you really want to stress the importance of making good choices and being self-disciplined.
Instructor or parent reads:

It's your future, not mine. I already went to school, made the decisions I needed in order to achieve my dreams, so that I can have the life I want. It's your turn. You can decide to do what you need to do, *or not*. It's your dreams, your life. I can't make you make the "right" choices. If you want to have a certain kind of life, you will have to make the choices yourself. I know you can do it. Working hard (practicing/studying/being self-disciplined) is difficult. But, when we work hard and make good decisions, we will receive great rewards later in life.

Journal 11 | Making Your Painting Come to Life

Instructor or parent journals:

Your child or student is in your painting. How will you plan your brushstrokes and the colors? When you make a mistake in your painting, how can you turn it into a work of art? How will you ensure that you will look upon your painting with pride and not regret?

STEP 12 | INSPIRE THEM TO OVERCOME SHYNESS

DO NOT NEGLECT THE SHY, QUIET TYPES

Most children will get past their shy feelings to interact with others, participate in class, and try something new. But for some, shyness can be so strong it can affect socialization and opportunities for growth, development, and enjoyment. In turn, this can affect self-efficacy and self-confidence.

In classrooms, the shy compliant students are easy to teach. We appreciate them because they allow us time and energy to work with other students. Older students, who are shy and private, may make us nervous, and we sometimes avoid them. Parents, teachers, and tutors, please be careful not to neglect our shy ones. Whether they are timid, reclusive, unresponsive, coy, or suspicious, what they all have in common are feelings of anxiety that should be addressed. We don't have to resolve their shyness, but they deserve our attempts to connect with them. By repeating a few sentiments over time, we can make a difference in their lives, which in turn will strengthen our classrooms and homes.

ADDRESS SHYNESS

Parents, tutors, and instructors can address shyness in the following ways.

- Have patience and understand that overcoming shyness is a process that takes time and courage.
- Communicate encouraging words. Plant seeds of thought that can grow in their brains over time.
- Avoid putting a spotlight on them, unless they've given you signs they are ready. You may want to say the next few suggestions privately and not in front of others. Or even better, address the entire class or family, not looking at anyone particular person.
- Tell them to not think about everything involved, just take the first step. Take one step at a time, even if it's backwards, we're learning, growing, and developing.
- Tell them it's okay to make a mistake, remind them that most of the time others aren't paying attention to what people are doing.
- Point out that most people are not as critical as we think. Ask, "Are you criticizing someone right now? Did you earlier today? Others aren't either."

- Tell them, "Be kind to yourself." Mention how we are our own worst critics. No one is perfect.
- Communicate that overcoming shyness takes practice.
- Communicate that overcoming shyness takes courage.
- Communicate that overcoming shyness takes time.
- Tell them that trying something new, making a new friend, trying out for a team, or joining a club may feel awkward and uncomfortable. But that's okay, because they are expanding their "circle" of knowledge.
- Listen actively, don't interrupt, and follow up by saying something like, "Good point."
- When they are scared or anxious, remind them to breathe and focus on something else. Looking up helps and can sometimes halt tears.
- Never push them to a breaking point. Give gentle nudges that say, "I can."
- Help them connect taking action to their successes.
- Have them read the characteristics of introverts and extroverts. Ask them if they think they are introverted or extroverted and why. Explain that the world needs both.
- Rather than yelling, use metaphors when they don't understand the importance and weight of what you're trying to say.

Lesson 12 | Shine

 For this activity you will need 2 identical birthday candles. Complete the following lesson with your child or classroom of students to inspire them to shine.
Instructor or parent reads the information on the left below:

Hold up 2 identical birthday candles.

These candles look a lot alike, don't they?

Turn the lights down.

Which candle is more beautiful? (You're looking for them to say, "They are the same.")

Light one of the candles.

Do the candles still look the same? (No)

Why? What's the difference? (Hopefully someone will say, "One is shining.")

Which one is more beautiful? (The one that's shining.)

Did you know that people can shine too? But most of us do not because we are shy. We are too shy to give that presentation, be in the play, run for student council, or even too shy to simply speak up!

Too often we are afraid that someone will criticize us. Sometimes you must defend your light. Do not be destroyed by another's criticism like a flickering flame is extinguished by a *thoughtless* gust of wind.

Blow out the candle.

Imagine if 20 people were in this room and only 2 or 3 of us were shining. How much more beautiful of a sight would it be to see all 20 of us shining?

When we are too shy to stand out and show the beauty within us, the world is a darker place. Sometimes people like us must practice the courage to shine. So, get out there, try your best, and shine.

Journal 12 | Address Shyness

 Instructor or parent journals:

Teachers, write down the names of your shy children and prepare a list of things you will think, say, and do for the whole class and for your shy students.

Parents, prepare a list of things you will think, say, and do with your child and the family.

STEP 13 | **BRIDGE THE DISTANCE**

BUILD A RELATIONSHIP WITH YOUR CHILD

Why do some parents have great relationships with their children, and some do not? Good parent-child connections don't just happen. All relationships take work and time. Like a marriage or a friendship, your relationship with your child is worthy of your attention, time, and focused energy.

But wait! There's so much to do. There's just not enough time, right? You will have a second chance at a job, but you will not get a second chance raising your child. Ninety percent of people on their deathbed say their biggest regret is that they didn't get closer to the people in their lives. And almost all parents wish they had spent more time with their kids. Can you guess how many said they wished they worked more?

So how do we make the time? Put your "4 rocks" first. Take a moment to review Step 5 Guide Them to Make Good Choices. In the lesson, we learned how our lives are less ruled by good and bad luck, and more by a *series* of choices. As we make choices, little by little, our lives begin to take shape in the direction we focus our energy. In other words, the choices and actions we make on a daily basis can determine how things will end up.

Likewise, the things we do (or don't do) every day are connected to our outcomes with our children. So, as we drive to the grocery store, watch TV, enforce chores and rules, help them with homework—in every interaction—we are creating the relationship we want (or do not want) to have with them. So, decide now. What do you want your relationship with your children to be like later in life? Where can you focus your precious and limited energy? What specific choices and actions can you take?

Children Learn What They Live

If children live with criticism, they learn to condemn.
If children live with hostility, they learn to fight.
If children live with ridicule, they learn to feel shy.
If children live with shame, they learn to feel guilty.
If children live with encouragement, they learn confidence.
If children live with tolerance, they learn patience.
If children live with praise, they learn appreciation.

If children live with acceptance, they learn to love.
If children live with approval, they learn to like themselves.
If children live with honesty, they learn truthfulness.
If children live with security, they learn to have faith in themselves
and in those about them.
If children live with friendliness, they learn the world is a nice place in which
to live.

BRIDGE THE DISTANCE WITH YOUR STUDENTS

Prevent Conflict Cycles

Conflict cycles can create distance between schools, students, and their families. They follow patterns that go something like this. The student experiences two or more bad things (e.g. student's parents fight at home and then he or she is embarrassed at school). The student responds (e.g. curses, talks back to the teacher, skips class). This provokes the teacher or staff to respond to the student (with words, body language, tone, actions). The adult's response at this point can trigger emotions to swell, causing the student to react with more negative behavior.

Don't Distance Yourself

When teachers, principals, staff members, parents, and students are caught in a conflict cycle, it can create distance between them. Some may wonder, what's wrong with keeping the distance? The problem with that is when you keep your distance from someone, it prevents you from developing feelings for that person. Likewise, that person will keep his or her distance and not develop feelings for you. When you don't care for someone, you are both more likely to respond in ways that will keep the cycle continuing to spin—breeding disrespect, lack of cooperation, mistrust, opposition, and defiance. A single teacher, principal, or counselor can completely disenfranchise a student.

Use Focus and Control to Break Out of Conflict Cycles

How can a teacher, school, or parent be successful when a conflict cycle exists? Conflict cycles can affect a student and family's well-being, a teacher's job satisfaction, and a school's academic performance. When teachers, principals, and staff shift their perspectives and energy towards focusing on ways to break conflict cycles, we will not only help bridge the distance between the students and school, but we will also improve grades and our school cultures.

It is up to one of the two people in a conflict cycle to respond in a way that will diffuse the other's emotional responses. In the case of a teacher and student, the adult will be the person who must avoid responding unfavorably to the student's behavior.

Control your verbal responses, body language, and tone. How? Resist the urge to judge or assume. Think or say to yourself, "Something else must be going on with this person." If you have to, imagine what else is going on at school or home. This can help shift your focus from judging to helping you stay calm and in control of what you say and do.

View and Communicate Disciplinary Actions as Opportunities to Learn and Improve

When it comes time for carrying out student consequences, include more than just punishments. When schools speak only of juvenile hall, alternative schools, and detention centers, they are limiting themselves and their students. Schools need to stop worshipping the volcano god of pain. Believing that suffering is the *only* way to teach someone a lesson is destructive. Academic and behavioral failures can also bring opportunities to learn and develop, Schools can produce healthier outcomes for students when their disciplinary actions are accompanied with communicating how mistakes and consequences are opportunities to learn

Provide Positive Reinforcement When They Deserve It

Some instructors are stingy with their compliments or provide them only to their "good" students. It might be difficult for many teachers to provide positive reinforcement to a student who has been sent to the office multiple times. The teacher may feel that giving positive reinforcement will affirm the "bad" things the student has done. He or she might also be afraid that complimenting or rewarding the student may send a message to classmates that the teacher is accepting the student's problem behaviors.

Teachers have the restorative power to break chronic patterns or not. One of the best ways to accomplish this is to provide positive reinforcement when students deserve it. Even the ones you don't "like." Be prepared to compliment certain students in private because comments may make some students feel uncomfortable, which can manifest in undesirable ways like responding with an unflattering comment to you. If that's the case, it's most likely because they don't trust you or anyone for that matter. You may not understand this; however, set aside your ego, practice patience, and attempt reinforcing their positive behavior again at a later time. It will likely spark a change and increase their trust in you, which can give rise to more positive attitudes and conduct.

BRIDGE THE DISTANCE WITH YOUR STUDENTS AND THEIR FAMILIES

Communicate with Parents Frequently

Teachers and staff often keep their distance from parents. This communicates to parents that the school administrator and teachers do not care. And, remember what happens when someone doesn't care? It makes people susceptible to respond in ways that can create conflict cycles. It's important for school staff members to make efforts to bridge the distance with the students' parents and families. Email brief weekly or monthly newsletters, call parents, reach out, and ask for their help. And most importantly, don't allow a conflict cycle to continue to spin. It will breed disrespect, lack of cooperation, mistrust, opposition, and defiance.

Diffuse Their Anger and Control Your Responses

It is up to one person in a conflict cycle to diffuse the other's emotional responses. It's going to have to start with you. So when you are confronted with a belligerent parent, what are you going to do? The first thing you should do is control your verbal responses, body language, and tone and refrain from judging. How? Think of why your parent could be angry. You don't have to know, just try to imagine what it could be, so that you're more equipped to empathize and respond in ways that don't keep the cycle spinning.

There are many reasons why parents can become angry. Here are some of the most common:

- The parents are ashamed of what their children have done.
- The parents feel powerless.
- Parents know what they're telling is true and you're just not listening or accepting the truth because of your hard-headed "objectivity."
- Parents have been to this rodeo before and they are sick and tired of being tossed around and trampled on and do not want the same thing to happen again. They may not have been mistreated at your school; it could have been another school.
- Something you're not aware of is going on in their lives (e.g. trauma, divorce, death, illness).

At times, parents of underperforming students can be quite hostile and may seem unwilling to listen and help. In order to get parents to listen and overcome hostility, you need to understand that they are not happy with their children's lack of success. The source of their anger and aggression is the embarrassment that their children are failing in your eyes (or one of the other reasons previously listed). They are frustrated, overwhelmed, and are at a loss for what to do. But, most parents want to help their children.

Refrain from Judging Students and Their Families

It is important for teachers and staff to realize they see only a snapshot of their students. Refrain from judging, because what you see, does not dictate who they will be. I say this respectfully, but it is not your job to pass judgment or to predict the future of your student. A lot of students come to a fork in the road during middle school and high school. Please do not escort them to the wrong path by judging, criticizing, and telling students they are criminals, delinquents, worthless, etc. These words and actions will incite them to choose the wrong way.

If you find it impossible to judge, ask yourself, "How are my thoughts and judging behaviors helping this person? What good is it doing?" Imagine someone is giving you a disapproving stare. It may, or may not, stop your behavior, and how does it make you feel? Defensive, spiteful, or offended? Or does it inspire you to change or be like the person who glared so judgmentally at you? Over time, what affect would repeated haughty, disdainful looks have on you? Might you become hostile, angry, depressed, apathetic, or rebellious?

Self-efficacy is a belief in one's ability to succeed. Underperforming students have a better chance of succeeding in school if they think they might be successful. A student needs to believe that he or she can do it. Think about a time when you were asked to perform what seemed like an impossible task that was beyond your skills. But, if you had a vision that one day you could do it, most likely, you were eventually able to do it. In the same way, self-efficacy can have the same influence on your students.

The key to developing self-efficacy in your students is to find ways to increase their motivation. Think of a time when you were in a job that you did not do well. Did you do better when your boss yelled at you or embarrassed you? Maybe at first you tried harder, but you just needed more support or training that could propel you to the level they expected. But if they just kept embarrassing you, your peers would see your failures. You might have become humiliated or changed jobs. Well, dear reader, it is the same for our students. And it is the same for their parents. Judging and embarrassing students and their families are de-motivators that demolish self-efficacy and keep the conflict cycle spinning.

Focus on What's in the Best Interest of the Child or Student

It can be challenging when discussions between administrators, teachers, and parents become heated debates. A parent, teacher, or administrator can stay out of the conflict cycle by asking each other out loud, "What is in the best interest of the child (or student)?" By asking this simple question, you can shift the goal of the conversation from winning the argument to focusing on correcting a problem.

Also, take a moment to analyze some of the programmed responses you say to parents. Are they in the best interest of the children? And is there any legal fiction you may be clutching on to? Does it help or prevent you from meeting the academic, behavioral, and emotional needs of your students?

Focusing on communicating, "what is in the best interests of your students" is a good way to keep your conversations with parents, teachers, and staff positive.

Partner with Parents, Tutors, and Mentors

One of the most powerful ways teachers can improve our students' behavioral, academic, emotional, linguistic, athletic, musical, and artistic successes is by partnering with parents. Schools can provide resources and opportunities to educate parents. When given tools, encouragement, and some inspiration, parents can affect student outcomes in a variety of ways. For example, parents of struggling students can be provided access to resources and materials to tutor their own children (or other children) in reading, study skills, test taking, behaviors, etc.

Ask yourself, "How am I inspiring my teachers *and parents* so they can encourage and inspire their students and children?" Progressive administrators and teachers understand that in order to increase the performance of their students, they will have to involve parents, tutors, and mentors in meaningful and significant ways.

Reach Out and Connect

An underperforming student has a higher chance of becoming successful if at least one parent, teacher, tutor, or school administrator consistently reaches out and connects with the student. It would be most effective if all these could come together, but it takes only one...you could be the one who creates the difference.

Lesson 13 | Choices and Actions Checklist

 Parents and family members can use this checklist to help bridge the distance and prevent a child or teen from becoming disenfranchised.

Help your child develop a close friendship with you, a mentor, peers, and family.

- Do things together. Spend longer chunks of time together. The only way your child will open up and start is if you are present.
- Spend time doing his or her hobbies. The reason your child may not want to spend time with you is because you are boring to them. Making time to do an activity that is interesting to them shows respect and acceptance and offers a way to connect with each other.
- Work together as a family to overcome difficulties.

- Make sure your child is not alone on a regular basis. Isolation builds walls, not relationships.
- Keep your child involved and in a positive environment, not texting and on Facebook. Set up chores, have them participate with family, and stay involved. Children will whine, but know that they will benefit, even if you feel as if you're not making a difference.

Teach goal setting.

- Help your child create checklists of responsibilities, goals, consequences, and rewards for reaching goals.
- Provide immediate positive reinforcement when you notice responsible behaviors.
- Involve your child in activities that create ownership.

Help develop good self-esteem.

- Give your child chances to shine.
- Give hugs and affection.
- Say, "I love you unconditionally" and mean it. Our children need to know that we still love them, even when they make mistakes. We may be angry, and we'll hold them accountable, but we still love them.
- Ask for your child's opinions.
- Listen, wait, and listen some more.
- When your child gets angry, don't take it personally. It's not about you. Besides, you're the adult, act like it.
- Express your desire for him or her to succeed.
- Read stories about people who fail and succeed.
- When a child shows signs of sadness, be positive and withhold criticisms. You may have to adjust your standards to encourage success.
- Build your child's trust in you by following through on your promises (e.g. picking him or her up when you say you will) and never shutting a child out when he or she needs you.
- Say, "I understand you are going through a difficult time and I want to find a way to help you through it." Talk about similar problems you faced and reassure your child you will stand by him or her.

 Instructors, counselors, coaches, tutors, and mentors:

Create a checklist of choices and actions you can take with your student. How can you bridge the distance and prevent them from becoming disenfranchised?

Journal 13 | Choices and Actions -> Outcomes

 Instructor or parent journals:

To a child, life is about making sure all 4 big rocks fit, not putting too many holes in the fence, and seeing $100 dollars every time they look in the mirror. And then getting through it all without their candle being snuffed out.

As we grow older, life begins to be about deeper concerns. We begin to wonder, *after I'm gone, what kind of difference did I make? What will remain of me in this world long after I'm gone?*

Review this unit and think about how you could bridge the distance between you and your child or student. Write down the areas you would like to focus? How could you reach out? What can you say, not say, or phrase things differently?

Write about how your decisions, choices, and actions directed your course in life? Where are you now because of the decisions, choices, and actions you've made? What would you like to achieve as you journey forward though life? And what parts of you would you like to remain in this world when you're no longer here? What decisions, choices, and actions can you take to help you reach these outcomes?

Figure 13.1   We Direct the Course of Our Lives

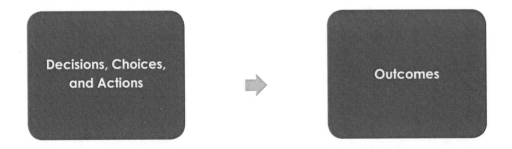

STEP 14 | **BUILD CHARACTER**

Fortify your child or students with reading, writing, and oral activities that inspire them to make healthy decisions, choices, and actions. Have your child or students read, write, and talk about people who have overcome obstacles.

Sources include:

- Magazine articles
- Aesop's Fables
- Tall tales, legends, mythology
- History, biographies
- Heroes, superhero movies
- Guinness Book of World Records
- Poetry, songs
- Theatre, movies
- Audio clips
- Pair nonfiction and fiction whenever possible (e.g. *Little House on the Prairie* with pioneer videos).

Reading to children in a specific manner can help students perform better on tests, writing assignments, spoken communication, and problem solving. Reading to children in the following manner can accomplish those and also improve: vocabulary, understanding inferences, making predictions, drawing conclusions, problem solving, and building moral fortitude.

When you're reading:

- Exercise word recognition and vocabulary.
  Ask, pointing to the word, "Do you know what that word means?" In school, a student is not likely to interrupt to ask the meaning of a word. At home, there are more opportunities and more time to talk about the meanings of words. Look up

definitions on an electronic device or have a pocket dictionary handy. Talk about what words mean from context clues or words in the story.

- Exercise comprehension.
  Main idea – Randomly and frequently ask, "What was the main idea of this paragraph (or page)?" If it's hard for them, you can help a student to more accurately find the main idea by asking, "What was the *single most* important thing this paragraph (or page) was about?"
  Summarize – Frequently ask them to summarize a chapter, unit, or story. If it's difficult, you can ask, "What happened in the beginning, middle, and end (of the chapter, unit, or story)?"

- Exercise the ability to predict.
  Ask, "What do you think will happen next?"

- Exercise the ability to understand inferences.
  Ask questions such as, "What do you think the main character meant when he did that?" Explain that an inference is an opinion formed based on an assumption or something that is implied.
  Example 1: "She slammed the door." = She must be mad.
  Example 2: "The abandoned car on the side of the road." = The car must be in need of repair.

- Exercise problem solving.
  Frequently ask, "Why do you think the character did that?" or "Why was that a good decision?" or "If the character chooses to ____ , what do you think the consequence will be?"

- Exercise moral fortitude.
  Ask, "Why was that a good/bad idea?"

FOLLOW READING COMPREHENSION, WRITTEN EXPRESSION, AND ORAL LANGUAGE ASSIGNMENTS WITH ACTIVITIES THAT FOCUS ON POSITIVE CHARACTER TRAITS

After reading articles, stories, and other inspirational literature, follow with an activity that will reinforce messages about positive character traits. Select writing and oral activities that can get students to think about the decisions, choices, and actions characters and real people can make.

Here are a few ideas:

- Summary (What happened in the beginning, middle, and end?)
- Character analysis (Describe a character based on what the character thinks, says, or does.)
- Theme (What was the lesson the author wanted a character or the reader to learn?)
- Find a main idea and supporting details
- Draw a conclusion or make an inference
- Find cause and effect
- Compare and contrast
- Find pros and cons
- Reader response (A student responds to what he or she read and writes about it - The most interesting thing I read was, I was surprised to learn, my favorite, I wonder)
- Write captions for pictures and photos
- Create a play based on a book, article, or movie

Make sure the activities you choose are interactive and appeal to visual, auditory, kinesthetic, and tactile learners. Periodically, have students pair up and read their work to each other. Give them opportunities to discuss healthy decisions, choices, and actions. Fellow students can provide and receive valuable feedback. They can also help generate ideas, problem solve, encourage, and support each other.

Have your child or students create an inspirational environmental print to display in your home or classroom. Publish their works on bulletin boards, a class website, in a book, and mount work on colored paper and display in a hallway. Give small rewards to students who get their work on the walls and update them with new student-made environmental print regularly. Have students present their work to parents during a Parent Night midyear. Also, ask students to brainstorm mottos for the class or your family and hang them on the wall.

FOLLOW WITH SPELLING AND VOCABULARY INSTRUCTION

Vocabulary and spelling instruction should relate to your character-building lessons. Many students, parents, and teachers do not know the definitions of important character traits or find it difficult to distinguish the difference between them. For example, many cannot verbalize the difference between honor and courage. That's why it is essential to show photos, real objects, and diagrams that help students learn and retain definitions.

Have students define some of the character traits and add them to their personal log of vocabulary and spelling words. English Language Arts students should have age-appropriate spelling and vocabulary tests covering character traits.

Use the list of character traits on the following page for ideas of words you can ask students to define.

We can describe a person (fictional or nonfictional) based on what a person thinks, says, and does. Based on their actions, thoughts, and speech we can analyze their character.

Figure 14.1   Character Traits: Words You Can Use to Describe Someone

Positive	Negative
Brave, courageous, heroic	Frightened, coward
Bold, fearless	Shy, timid
Responsible, reliable, protective, caring	Careless, reckless, thoughtless
Confident	Unconfident, uncertain
Leader	Gullible
Determined	Stubborn
Energetic, hard-working	Lazy, sluggish
Tenacious	Inflexible, yielding, fragile, frail
Cooperative	Disagreeable, mischievous, naughty
Caring, considerate, thoughtful	Thoughtless, demanding
Empathetic	Apathetic, detached, clueless
Respectful	Rude, disrespectful
Unselfish, generous, thrifty	Selfish, greedy
Cheerful, joyful, humorous	Gloomy, serious, dismal, mournful
Sane, rational, healthy, lucid	Demented, disturbed, unbalanced
Prepared, careful, cautious	Unprepared, careless, reckless
Witty, clever, resourceful	Slow, sluggish
Creative, imaginative, inventive	Dull, generic
Curious, adventurous	Homely
Calm, peaceful	Wild, nervous, obnoxious, thunderous
Humble	Conceited, proud, vain, prideful
Attractive, stunning, lovely	Grotesque, monstrous
Satisfied	Desperate
Good, honest, truthful, loyal	Evil, corrupt, foul, wicked, dishonest

FREQUENTLY PROVIDE JOURNAL OPPORTUNITIES

Provide students with the opportunity to journal on a regular basis. Journaling can help children and teens anticipate and think through different scenarios. More importantly, take the time to write them back. Keep it concise. Do not write judgments. Simply make a comment or ask a question that will help them explore the situation and gain more perspective. Make questions or comments that will help them become more insightful and increase their awareness of decision-making and responsibilities.

Here are a few ideas for writing/discussion prompts:

- Write about a family member and what makes that person special.
- Write about why mistakes are necessary.
- Write about the nicest thing that happened to you today (or yesterday).
- Think of a way you could help another person now or in the future.
- What do you need to live? What do you need to be happy?
- What are nice gifts you could give that do not cost money?
- What are some chores that must be done at home? What does someone need to know in order to do them? What if they didn't get done?
- Ask an adult about their regular bills and expenses. Ask what a budget is. Who uses them and why? Write what you learn.
- Decide on a project you would like to do. What steps do you need to take? What materials would you need? What do you need to prepare?
- What careers look interesting to you? Search on the Internet what you need to know to have a job like that? What do you need to do to keep a job?
- Watch a TV program, video clip, or movie. What smart or unwise decisions did a character make? What did the person need to make a good decision? Would you have done the same? Or would you have done something different? Why?
- Write about safety in our homes. What steps can we take to ensure everyone is safe in our homes? Why is this important?

Gardeners know that they can't make plants grow. Plants grow themselves. Gardeners provide the right conditions for that to happen. Good gardeners understand those conditions. Running a school or teaching a class or raising a family is much more like gardening than like engineering. It's about providing the best conditions for growth and development. And if we get that right we'll see an abundant harvest of talent, commitment, imagination and creativity in all of our children and in all of our schools.

Ken Robinson (Fifield, 2012, p 35)

Lesson 14 | Overcoming Obstacles

 Instructor or parent can find books or articles on the Internet with your child or students about inspirational people who have overcome their obstacles.

Find books or articles on the Internet with your child or student about an inspirational person who has overcome their obstacles. I highly recommend reading about Wilma Rudolph or Wendy Booker.

Ask the student to summarize what they read. (Summary - What happened in the beginning, middle, and end?)

Then ask your child or students to read through Figure 14.1 Character Traits: Words You Can Use to Describe Someone. Ask, "What words would you use to describe Wilma Rudolf, Wendy Booker, or the other person you choose? What did Wilma or Wendy think, say, or do to make you choose those words to describe her?"

Note: Many students, even older ones, do not know the meanings of words like courage, tenacious, and dismal, so have a dictionary handy.

Journal 14 | Activities that Inspire Healthy Decisions, Choices, and Actions

 Instructor or parent journals:

Review the suggestions in this step and write about the different reading, writing, oral, and visual activities you could use to inspire your child or student to make healthy decisions, choices, and actions.

STEP 15 | **BE RELEVANT**

MOTIVATE BY BEING CULTURALLY RESPONSIVE

Culturally responsive teaching is a sociocultural approach to teaching, based on the work of Russian psychologist Lev Vygotsky. It "encourages students to learn by building on the experiences, knowledge, and skills they bring to the classroom" (Hughes, 2005, p 3).

Take a moment to think how we learn a new concept or skill we haven't learned before. We are more likely to comprehend, retain, and recall newly learned information when we relate the new information to a similar concept or skill we already know. For example, students who have a general understanding of soccer will comprehend, recall, and retain more details from a story about soccer than students who have never seen a soccer game before. When they relate, it is relevant. It's one way teachers, tutors, and parents, can help our children bridge new knowledge to meaningful aspects of their lives. This can help and motivate our students who suffer from poor short-term and working memory or come from culturally or linguistically diverse backgrounds or students who say they "can't" or "don't care."

Culturally responsive teaching also includes providing positive cultural and linguistic perspectives and reshaping the curriculum to include positive contributions of cultures (Hughes, 2005).

> Culture encompasses more than nationality or race; rather, it is a layered network that includes beliefs, ideas, behaviors, communication styles, and thought processes. Culture influences the way individuals approach and process information—like a lens, which shapes how each one of us, views the world.
>
> Matthew DeMario

When I was working on my Master's in Education at The University of Texas, I was assigned to co-teach 6th grade Math students during summer school. One of our projects during our teaching internship was to incorporate culturally responsive teaching into our experience. Most of the interns chose to incorporate positive aspects about African American, Hispanic, and Asian cultures into their lessons. In this way, the students could see their races in their instruction. However, I wanted to provide culturally diverse perspectives that included my students' languages, norms, values, behaviors, and attitudes, since those are part of culture also. I felt if I included those, then my students would see themselves in the lessons even more.

What follows is a *creative, fun, fast, and efficient* way I was able to get my 6th grade students to share *their* norms, values, and perspectives with me on the first day of class. I also describe how I used the information in my math lessons and the motivational effects it had on my students.

On the first day of class, I introduced my cultural self to my students with a verbal Cultural Quiz. I read aloud the first question, "What is my favorite food?" I gave them 3 multiple-choice answers and asked them to guess what they thought the correct answer was: a) Taco Bell, or b) my mom's homemade soups, or c) sushi. As I shared the answer to each question, I started to reveal my cultural self to my students. Soon, I began to witness how my new students enjoyed seeing me as a human, a person who has interests, a past, and a life.

Example

Here's the quiz I interactively shared with my students on the first day of school.

Figure 15.1 My Cultural Quiz (Laurie Hunter, 2014)

1. What is my favorite food?
a) Taco Bell Burrito Supreme
b) My mom's homemade soups
c) Sushi *
*My sons are ¼ Japanese. Their dad's mom, their grandmother, was born and raised in Japan. At 13, my sons learned how to prepare sushi. We make it frequently and it is my favorite!
2. What is my favorite movie?
a) Star Wars movies
b) The Hundred-Foot Journey about a family who leaves India for France and open a restaurant*
c) Harry Potter movies
*The Hundred-Foot Journey is about family, India, France, cooking, and overcoming challenges. Wow!
3. What is my favorite hobby?
a) Spending time on Facebook
b) Taking walks in nature
c) Reading How To Books *

*I am dyslexic, and I didn't learn how to read until 2nd grade. I learned just because you're not good at something now, doesn't mean it will always be that way. I didn't start out being a good reader, but now I am. Plus, I teach children how to become better readers, and I read How To Books for fun!

4. If I could learn a new skill or talent, what would it be?

a) Mountain climbing in the cloud forests of South America and the monsoon forests of Australia

b) Deep sea exploration, studying the habitats and behavior of the blue-ringed octopus

c) Playing the guitar *

*I'd never learned to play an instrument. At the age of 37, I finally took guitar lessons.

5. If I could meet any person (real or fictional), who would it be and why?

a) Benjamin Franklin

b) Harry Potter

c) My great, great, great grandmother, Mary Summerline who lived from 1853 to 1945*

*My grandma collected photos and records of relatives who lived in our family. When my grandma told me stories about my great, great, great grandmother, Mary Summerline, she reminded me of me, and that makes me want to meet her.

6. Who is my hero and why?

a) Martin Luther King, Jr., because he was a strong man who used his intellect and his words to fight for what is right. *

b) My 10th and 11th grade English teacher for believing in my potential. *

c) My mom for modeling and teaching me to be resourceful and strong and for expecting nothing but the best from me. *

*If you think my hero is Martin Luther King, Jr., my teacher, or my mom—they all correct, because they are all my heroes. Martin Luther King is my hero because he used his words and his intellect to stand up for what was right. I admire him greatly for that. I also admire my high school English teacher. She saw how I struggled and responded. She saw my potential and encouraged me. She is a good friend to me today. My mom is also my hero because she modeled to me how to be resourceful and how to protect and defend myself. Something else I thank her for is that she expected the best from me. Because of her, I am the strong and resourceful person I am today.

Afterwards, I explained to the students that it was their turn to share. I gave each student the following quiz. It contains six questions with a space for them to write three possible answers. I read each question, one at a time. I asked them to write three possible answers, but one had to be correct. I walked around and heard them think out loud and share with each other. I gave the students about five minutes to write their multiple-choice answers. I told them to star or circle the correct answer. I explained to the class, I would not reject their responses or think any less of them for the same reason I wouldn't have wanted them to reject my responses and think less of me for the quiz I created.

That evening, I read my students' quizzes and thought of ways I could incorporate the info into my lessons. My students' quizzes provided me with names of the most contemporary TV shows, video games, sports stars, entertainers, movies, heroes, and cherished family members and events that were relevant and meaningful to them. That evening, I created my lessons with decimal and percent problems using some of their responses, such as target practice, basketball, and soccer. I also came up with ratio problems using nachos, grandmas, quinceañeras, and bar mitzvahs.

Each day, I mentioned information from their Cultural Quizzes. The students responded so favorably; it incited me to use this significant, valuable, and meaningful information. I incorporated as much as I could. It made what I had to say more relevant.

As I strived to get to know my students, I realized the Cultural Quiz was a gateway to achieving a more meaningful relationship with my students. It kick-started the process of getting to know them. For instance, Jesiah answered the question, "If you could meet any person who would it be?" he wrote the names of his favorite soccer players: David Beckham (England), Christiano Ronaldo (Portugal), and Ronaldinho Gaucho (Brazil). During class, when I used them in an example, I glanced to witness a bright light flash in his face. Soon after, I discovered Jesiah was a talented soccer player who loved to watch World Cup competitions.

A few days later, I was explaining to my students how to find equivalent ratios. I said, "When Tupac was alive, his band had 1 drummer who used 2 drumsticks for 5 drums. If T.I. and Akon played in a concert together and both their drummers used the same number of drumsticks and drums that Tupac's band used, how many would there be?" Several hands excitedly rose into the air to answer. Next, I asked, "If Beyonce and her drummer joined them, what would the ratio of drumsticks to drums be?" Xavion raised his hand with what I assumed would be the answer. Instead, he responded, "Ma'am, you are a fine teacher."

> I don't think I've ever met a child who wasn't motivated to figure things out, to find the answers to personally relevant questions. However, I've met (and taught) plenty of kids who aren't motivated to sit quietly and listen to someone else talk or to memorize the definitions of a list of words.

Name _____

Quiz

1. What is my favorite food?

a)

b)

c)

2. What is my favorite movie?

a)

b)

c)

3. What is my favorite hobby?

a)

b)

c)

4. If I could learn a new skill or talent, what would it be?

a)

b)

c)

5. If I could meet any person (real or fictional), who would it be *and why*?

a)

b)

c)

6. Who is my hero and *why*?

a)

b)

c)

Without the quizzes, I could not have learned my students' personal cultural information so quickly. On the first day of class I learned from shy Marquilies that his hero is his grandma, because without her he would have failed 1st, 2nd, or 3rd grade. I have learned that playful Migos's heroes are his parents because they always told him, "I could do it." I also learned that if Xavion could meet any person, "it would be God, because with Him anything is possible."

Another quiz question was, "If you could learn a new skill or talent, what would it be?" Joshe's response was "Math." On the last day of class, a few minutes after all the students had left, Joshe walked back into the classroom. My co-teacher and I were touched when he said he had to come back to tell us thank you, that he really enjoyed our class, and that he learned so much from us. He looked as if he wanted to hug us. For me, it's times like these that remind me of what teaching is all about.

My experiences and research validate how learning our students' cultures can help instructors positively affect our students' behaviors and narrow achievement gaps (Hughes, 2005, p 52). There is a connection between practicing culturally responsive teaching and our students' academic success. My students' progress monitoring data showed that every student progressed and not a single student failed our class. Moreover, on the final day of summer school, my co-teacher and I were surprised at our realization that we did not have to take disciplinary action with any student. We did not have one single power struggle, no resistance, not even one hostile word or action from our students. Our disciplinary struggles were limited to minor infractions, such as goofing off and excessive talking.

The Cultural Quiz can serve as a vehicle for you to develop your cultural competence. Mestas and Petersen define cultural competence as "Having the evolving knowledge and skills used for maintaining a process to increase one's respect, understanding and knowledge of the similarities and differences between one's self and others. This includes the values, lifestyles, abilities, beliefs and opportunities that influence every aspect of how people relate to each other" (Mestas & Peterson, 1999).

When you mention aspects of your child's or students' cultures, you and what you say will become relevant and meaningful. Why should you go through the trouble? What's in it for you?

- You will grab the attention of the students who "don't care."
- You will make assignments a little more bearable or interesting for those students who "can't" do it.
- More students will retain what you're teaching, so you won't have to repeat yourself quite so much.
- You can integrate your students' interests and culture into their math problems, writing assignments, and other learning activities. It will add interest to their assignments and motivate the entire class.

- More students will succeed academically and behaviorally and, in turn, you will earn more respect, cooperation, and success.

Step 19 provides more detail about how we can cultivate cultural intelligence.

Lesson 15 | Cultural Quiz

 Instructor or parent can complete the following lesson with your child or students to share cultural information with each other. Teachers can incorporate the interests and cultures of their underperforming students into assignments, so they will be more relatable and relevant.

Create your own cultural quiz and ask your child or students to guess the correct answers. Be prepared to share your answers with interesting details about yourself.

Afterwards, provide your child or students with a copy of the quiz questions. Ask them to create their own multiple-choice answers on their quiz. Tell them to draw a star next to the correct answer. If they don't want to write their own quiz, then interview them and write down or type their responses.

Journal 15 | How Will You Be More Relevant?

 Instructor or parent journals:

Reflect on your child or students' quiz responses and write how you will use this valuable information in your daily lessons, homework, and tests. Contemplate how each will increase your relevance and motivate them. For example, Math teachers can incorporate people, places, and things that their students value into fraction, ratio, slope, and percent word problems. This could create more interesting homework assignments and tests. French teachers could ask students to participate in various discussions in French, such as could you live without your phone for 24 hours? This could motivate them to practice their verbal communication skills and increase their desire to participate in class.

STEP 16 | IDENTIFY THE OBSTACLES PREVENTING SUCCESS

UNDERSTAND THE ROOT CAUSE OF YOUR CHILD'S DIFFICULTIES

When students are struggling in school, it is important to understand the root cause of their difficulties. "Lazy" and "doesn't care" are not root causes. If you do not already know the underlying, fundamental cause, start creating documentation that will lead you to why academic, behavioral, or social breakdowns are occurring.

Any teacher or parent can use this same approach. Whether you are a French teacher with students suffering from an inability to memorize vocabulary and conjugate verbs or a Math teacher with students who break down during word problems, you can use Step 16 to help you identify the obstacles preventing their success.

CREATE A BRIEF SUMMARY OF HISTORY

Parents and teachers who would like to identify obstacles and root causes for a child or student's difficulties can begin by reviewing report cards, notes from conferences, and other forms of communication to create a brief summary of the student's school history. If you are a tutor, coach, or mentor with limited access to reports, you can ask a parent to supply you with relevant history.

ATTEND PARENT TEACHER CONFERENCES

Much can be gained by attending parent-teacher conferences every time they're offered. Conferences build a connection between school and home. Teachers and parents build a rapport. Moreover, parents and teachers learn from each other. Parents should ask teachers the following questions below and in Figure 16.1. Likewise, teachers, tutors, coaches, and mentors can ask the following questions to themselves regarding their student(s).

Figure 16.1   Questions to Ask During Parent-Teacher Conferences

What are my child's strengths and weaknesses?

Describe his biggest challenges? Describe what the problem(s) look like?

What do you attribute his or her low grade to? What difficulties have you observed that contribute?

What do you think the root cause for his difficulties could be?

How do you think I can address his difficulties as a parent?

How can you address his difficulties as a teacher? Does the school offer screening, tutoring, mentoring, or counseling services?

REVIEW SUMMARY OF HISTORY AND CONFERENCE NOTES TO FIND KEYWORDS

After you have created a brief summary of school history and notes from your conference(s), search through them to find keywords. Afterwards, you will use the keywords to research and learn more about your child or student's difficulties.

Example

Vet is 9 years old and in the 4th grade. His mother scanned past report cards and notes. She wrote a brief summary of Vet's school history (below). Afterwards, Vet's mother searched through the summary she had compiled for keywords that described her son's most notable difficulties and strengths. Then, she underlined the keywords in the following manner.

In Kindergarten, my son, Vet, had a really difficult time learning to read. Towards the end of the year, he was <u>placed in a reading "club"</u> with five other students who also weren't reading. They were <u>given extra reading and writing instruction</u> three days a week. Vet's teacher told me she thought he was delayed because "he was <u>very active</u> and less mature than the other students." Vet loved his Kindergarten teacher and school, even though it was very hard for him. At home, I tried every day to get my son to read with me, but he just wasn't interested.

In 1st grade, Vet <u>received additional reading, writing, and spelling instruction</u> from a reading support specialist. He finally learned to read, but <u>his reading was inaccurate and sounded slow and choppy.</u>

In 2nd grade, his grades improved, and he was not pulled out to receive any additional instruction. However, I had to help him with his homework, or it did not get done. It <u>would take him at least an hour to complete his homework.</u> He would tell me he didn't like school. He was sick often and missed 10 days of school.

In 3rd grade, Vet made passing grades, but his teacher reported he was <u>below grade-level in reading, spelling, and written expression.</u> He attended <u>after school tutoring</u> that targeted students who were at risk of failing the mandatory state tests. He barely passed the state reading and math tests.

Now, Vet is in 4th grade and he is struggling more than ever. It seems like he has <u>problems in every subject.</u> He <u>gets upset every time he works on writing assignments</u>, especially book reports. His Math teacher reported, "Vet still <u>hasn't memorized his addition and multiplication facts</u>, and it's affecting his attitude and grades." He suggested I hire a tutor and I just did. I drive him to see an intervention tutor two times a week for reading, spelling, and math. I'm afraid he is <u>at risk of being retained.</u>

Vet's mother had brought the set of questions to ask during Parent-Teacher Conferences in Figure 16.1 to Vet's current 4th grade Reading and Math teachers. She took notes at the conference, and here's her summary of what was said during their conference. Next, Vet's mom searched through her notes from the parent-teacher conference and underlined the following keywords.

What are my child's strengths and weaknesses?

Both teachers reported that my son, Vet, is a "good" student when he tries. He can be <u>creative</u> at times and he does well for his Art teacher. She showed me some of his <u>doodling</u> on an assignment. His <u>weakest subject is reading, but he's starting to struggle in math.</u>

Describe his biggest challenges? Describe what the problem(s) look like?

His Reading teacher said Vet's <u>reading fluency rate and reading comprehension were very low</u>, so he reads slower than most of the students in his grade. She also mentioned that she stopped calling on him to read out loud, because she noticed <u>he makes frequent errors</u> and gets <u>embarrassed often when he's reading.</u> His Math teacher mentioned Vet still <u>hasn't memorized his multiplication tables,</u>

which is affecting his performance in division, <u>word problems</u>, and <u>sequencing</u> in multi-step problems.

What do you attribute his or her low grade to? What difficulties have you observed that contribute?

Both teachers agreed that he struggles mostly with daily work. It <u>takes him a long time</u> and then he has to rush at the end to turn it in. The Reading teacher said she thinks he would do better if he didn't get <u>distracted</u> and would focus on his work. Sometimes he <u>gets in trouble "goofing off</u> with a couple of the other active kids in class."

Both teachers mentioned he completes his homework and gets good grades on homework. I had to interrupt to tell them it's because I <u>have to spend hours with him, helping him with his assignments</u>. I told the teachers <u>how hard it was for him to write</u> his biography report and essay describing Newton's Three Laws of Motion. I told them how it made him <u>cry</u> and <u>every day is a struggle</u> and I know there is something wrong.

What do you think the root cause for his difficulties could be?

The Reading teacher thinks Vet's "a <u>bright</u> boy, just <u>active</u> and would rather be outside playing." She feels he's not applying himself as well as he could. I told her that he wants to do well, but school is beating him down and it is <u>affecting his confidence.</u>

How do you think I can address his difficulties as a parent?

I told them I've <u>hired an academic intervention tutor</u>, and she is helping me figure out the root causes for his difficulties and to help him become more successful and confident.

How can you address his difficulties as a teacher? Does the school offer screening, tutoring, mentoring, or counseling services?

I asked the teachers if there was anything more they, or the school, could do. I specifically asked if the school would screen my son for dyslexia. The Reading teacher said she's doing the best she can. She conceded to documenting some of the issues she's observed and will request that the school screen him for <u>dyslexia, orthographic processing deficits, dysgraphia, and ADHD.</u>

ANSWER THREE GUIDING QUESTIONS WHEN RESEARCHING ACADEMIC CHALLENGES

Now that you have identified keywords related to your child's or student's difficulty from the student's history and parent teacher conference, you are ready to begin your research. During your search, use the following three guiding questions to help you gain an understanding of the fundamental causes of your child's difficulties, the processes involved, and relationships of skills.

Figure 16.2   Use Keywords to Research Academic Challenges

Guiding Question 1: What could the underlying, fundamental cause(s) be?

Guiding Question 2: What are basic processes involved to do the desired task correctly?

Guiding Question 3: What skills are related? What skills depend on other skills?

Example

Here's how Vet's mother used the three guiding questions to learn more and understand her son's difficulties in reading.

Guiding Question 1: What could the underlying, fundamental cause(s) be?

Vet's mother found reputable sources on the Internet such as research studies, university and .gov websites, and books. She found that the fundamental causes for Vet's reading problems most likely stem from difficulties with decoding, phonemic awareness, reading fluency, and comprehension.

Guiding Question 2: What are basic processes involved to do the desired task correctly?

Vet's mother studied the process involved when a new reader learns to read. Even though her son was in 4th grade and he "knew" how to read, she felt she needed to understand the basic process of reading from the perspective of a beginner reader. Here's what she learned.

New readers blend phonemes to read words. For example, the word *shell* contains three phonemes, /sh/ /e/ /l/, even though there are 5 letters. The three sounds blend to produce the word *shell*. Beginner readers rely on their knowledge of phonics to decode letters and sound out new words until they are able to recognize them. Decoding words requires learning how strings of letters form strings of sounds (phonemes) to form words.

More specifically, new readers decode by sounding out the first letter or letter group by converting it to its corresponding speech sound (sound-symbol correspondence). Next, they move to the right (directionality) and blend the first sound with the next sound (blending). Then they continue in the same manner with the following sounds. Beginner readers repeat those sounds at the rate of speech to hear the word. When sound-symbol correspondence, directionality, and blending are performed automatically, then automaticity is achieved (Hallahan et al, 2005).

Vet's mom could, now, see how difficulties with the basic process of decoding affects other fundamental skills, such as comprehension (understanding), and reading fluency (rate and accuracy).

Guiding Question 3: What skills are related? What skills depend on other skills?

Decoding, phonemic awareness, reading fluency, and comprehension are all related. Vet's mom found the following information, which describes how all four skills are connected and how problems in any of these areas could be affecting her sons' reading and comprehension abilities:

- **Phonemic Awareness and Phonics Affect Decoding**

You can tell when a not-so-new-reader struggles with decoding. When he or she reads, it will sound choppy (dysfluent) and the student will make 3 or more errors every 60 seconds of reading. We can help a student become a more fluent and accurate decoder by strengthening the student's phonemic awareness and knowledge of letter-sound relationships.

Figure 16.3   Skills Needed for Beginning Readers to Decode Words

Phonemic awareness is not phonics. Rather, it is the ability to hear, identify, and manipulate the individual sounds in words (Eunice Kennedy Shriver NICHHD, 2001, p 1). "Effective phonemic awareness instruction teaches children to notice, think about, and work with (manipulate) sounds in spoken language" (p 4). "**Phonics** instruction teaches children the relationships between the letters (graphemes) of written language and the individual sounds (phonemes) of spoken language" (p 11).

It is important to note that the difference between skilled and unskilled beginner readers is not an issue of intelligence or motivation. The difference lies in how well a child can break down words into phonic chunks and convert those chunks into sounds.

- **Phonemic Awareness and Phonics Affect Reading Comprehension**
Not only is phonic (letter-sound) knowledge important for decoding, but also for comprehension. Eighty percent of the variance in first grade reading comprehension can be attributed to the students' knowledge of the letters (and letter groups) and mapping them to their corresponding sounds, so that readers can sound out until they recognize words (Foorman et al, 1997). If a student has trouble recognizing letters, letter groups, and their sounds, it will affect their decoding skills. Consequently, poor decoders will devote more of their working memory to decoding words and less on comprehending what they are reading (Rayner et al, 2001). This explains how students' challenges with accuracy (reading the word "fog" instead of "frog" or "for" instead of "from" or "casual" instead of "causal") can impact their comprehension.

- **Phonemic Awareness and Phonics Affect Reading Fluency**
Additionally, students (in second grade and above) who lack phonemic and phonic awareness typically struggle decoding words. This negatively affects reading fluency. Reading fluency is the ability to read swiftly, accurately, and with expression. A dysfluent reader reads slower, sounds choppy, pauses more frequently, reads fewer correct words per minute (CWPM), and may lack expression while reading. A dysfluent reader takes more time and energy to read words, making it more challenging for the reader to get joy and meaning out of what was read. Low reading fluency rates and errors can often lead to poor reading comprehension. This impacts our students' ability to understand and recall what they read in class and for homework. When the root causes of poor comprehension are not addressed, they can have a negative impact on students' academic, social, and emotional competencies, as well as their behavior, grades, and self-confidence.

CREATE A DIAGRAM TO SEE RELATIONSHIPS AND IDENTIFY WEAK SKILLS

Review what you have learned from your research. Determine how your child or teen's weakest area relates to various prerequisite skills. Use arrows to show how one competency can directly affect another.

Example

Here's the diagram Vet's mother created to show what skills depend on other skills and how they can affect each other.

Figure 16.4   Skilled Reading and Behavior Depend on Other Skills

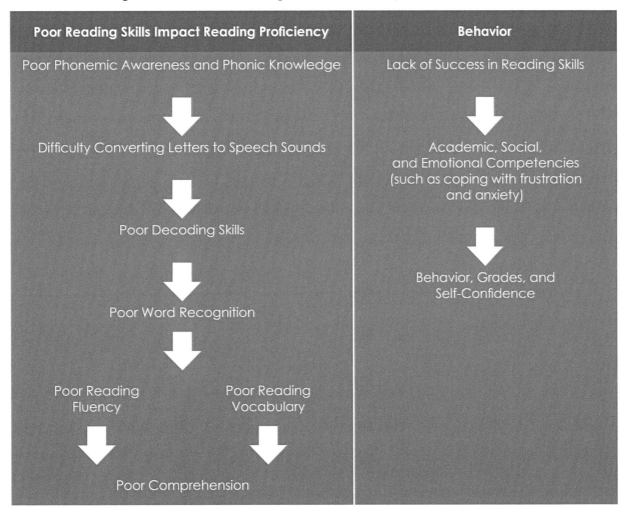

Poor Reading Skills Impact Reading Proficiency	Behavior
Poor Phonemic Awareness and Phonic Knowledge	Lack of Success in Reading Skills
⬇	⬇
Difficulty Converting Letters to Speech Sounds	Academic, Social, and Emotional Competencies (such as coping with frustration and anxiety)
⬇	⬇
Poor Decoding Skills	Behavior, Grades, and Self-Confidence
⬇	
Poor Word Recognition	
⬇	
Poor Reading Fluency Poor Reading Vocabulary	
⬇ ⬇	
Poor Comprehension	

To summarize: Lack of **phonemic awareness and phonic knowledge** affects a student's ability to map the sounds that letters and letter groups make. This prevents a student from remembering the sounds that letters and letter groups make and from retrieving them accurately and automatically. This affects the student's ability to efficiently **convert letters to their corresponding speech sounds**. **Poor decoding skills** affects the student's ability to recognize words. **Poor word recognition** may limit a student's **reading vocabulary** and slow down the student's **reading fluency rate** (how swiftly and accurately they read). The reader who devotes more of their working memory to figuring out vocabulary and reading fluently has less for comprehending what they are reading. This, as a result, can affect **comprehension**.

Lack of success in reading skills can affect a student's **academic, social, and emotional competencies** such as coping with frustration and anxiety. These, in turn, can affect a student's **behavior, grades, and self-confidence**.

Instructors and parents of students with ADHD, dyslexia, dysgraphia, and autism (who are not proficient readers, writers, or spellers), it is essential to your students' success that you are familiar with the concepts in this step. If you are not, I highly recommend that you read *Put Reading First: The Research Building Blocks for Teaching Children to Read*. Currently, it is available for free.

Lesson 16 | Productive Parent and Teacher Conferences

Parents, ask your child's teacher what specific things he or she can do to make better grades. "Try harder" and "work harder" are not specific enough. You need to know specifically what can be done in order to make grades and behaviors improve in the desired areas. Subsequently, use this information to guide your research to understand your child's difficulties.
Teachers, who are reading this, can also ask themselves these questions regarding an underperforming student.

During the parent-teacher conference, ask questions in this order to get specific information.

What are my child's strengths and weaknesses?

Describe his or her biggest challenges? (daily work, homework, test-taking) Describe what the problem looks like to you.

What do you attribute his or her low grade to? What difficulties have you observed that contribute? (e.g. test anxiety, distracted, failing to turn in homework, reluctance, avoids assignments or activities)

What do you think the root cause of his or her difficulties could be? Why is he or she anxious with testing/reading/writing/math, distracted, reluctant to do work, not applying him or herself, not focused, etc.?

How do you think I can address that as a parent? How do you as a teacher?

Does the school offer screening, tutoring, mentoring, or counseling services?

*Remember to take notes. If you disagree, have the courage to speak up, and do it respectfully with tact. Save your strong reactions until you can process the information. Advocate for what you know to be true. You will be more effective if you 1) do not get emotional and 2) speak matter-of-factly.

> Courage is what it takes to stand up and speak; courage is also what it takes to sit down and listen.

> Winston Churchill

Journal 16 | Getting to the Root Cause

 Instructor or parent journals:

Reflect on the ways you would like to see your child or a student improve. In order to stimulate improvement, you need to put your attention and energy towards *specific* areas and take conscious actions that will achieve results. You cannot expect to address a wound on your leg if you put a bandage on your arm. You've got to put the bandage where it needs to be in order to make a difference, otherwise the wound will continue to cause more intense pain, become infected, or affect other parts of the body. Also, if you continually keep getting hurt, you would want to address the source of what is causing the wounds, rather than constantly putting on more bandages. Likewise, before you can figure out how to remove roadblocks and obstacles, you must first identify the root cause(s) of your child's difficulty.

Reflect on the responses from Lesson 16 Productive Parent and Teacher Conferences. Use the information to begin your research.

Answer the three guiding questions when researching difficulties.

Guiding Question 1: What could the underlying, fundamental cause(s) be?
Guiding Question 2: What are basic processes involved to do the desired task correctly?
Guiding Question 3: What skills are related? What skills depend on other skills?

Then create a diagram to see relationships and identify weak skills. This will prepare you for the next step, removing obstacles preventing success.

STEP 17 | **REMOVE THE OBSTACLES PREVENTING SUCCESS**

UNDERSTAND HOW THE RIGHT INSTRUCTION CAN REMOVE OBSTACLES

After completing Step 16 Identify the Obstacles Preventing Success, you should have 1) gained a better understanding of the underlying, fundamental causes of your child or student's difficulties, 2) outlined the processes involved to do the desired task correctly, and 3) made a diagram of relationships to see how fundamental skills can impact other academic and behavioral competencies. This should help you pinpoint where the breakdowns are occurring and obstacles that are preventing your child's or student's success. Now you are ready for the next step, removing obstacles that prevent academic and behavioral success.

Just like a Band-Aid cannot last an entire school career, neither can "Band-Aid" approaches and solutions. It's time to remove the bandages and address the source of what's causing the pain (for everyone). Knowing the root cause for your child's or student's difficulties will expand your insight. It will also help you become more patient, improve communication with key people, and help you become an effective advocate. This can relieve some of the stress struggling students feel. Knowing and addressing the root cause of his or her difficulties can help you figure out what may be the reason for misbehaviors, lack of respect, and unwillingness to cooperate. Knowing the root cause can help you figure out what is the right instruction for a child.

Believe it or not, one of the biggest obstacles that may be preventing your child or student from achieving success is the type of instruction they are currently receiving. On page one of this book, I share my twin sons' battle with learning how to read. The following excerpt is from my journal when I discovered that the "help" I had been giving them was one of their obstacles!

You hear it all the time, "Successful readers read to their parents every night." TRANSLATION: "Non-dyslexic readers read to their parents every night." Many teachers and parents do not understand the difficulties and pain associated with students who struggle learning to read. Many get on their high horse touting how important it is for your child to read to you every day. Those teachers and parents have no idea what we go through, the tears, the shame, the exasperation, over and over. It's no wonder we quit. We begin to think we're doing more harm than good by forcing our struggling readers to read.

And, you know what? I *was* doing more harm than good! By the time I journaled that entry, I had started my research and began to realize that making struggling dyslexic children read more is not how you get them to become proficient readers. Asking them to read more, when they didn't have the basic and fundamental skills, made things worse. If I had not done my research, his teachers and I would have kept providing them with the wrong type of instruction. I had witnessed how proper reading intervention was way more beneficial. Without intervention, making them read more was an obstacle preventing their success in reading, spelling, and written expression.

ANSWER THREE GUIDING QUESTIONS WHEN RESEARCHING INTERVENTIONS

The previous chapter, Step 16 Identify the Obstacles Preventing Success, explains how parents, teachers, tutors, counselors, and coaches can uncover and identify keywords from a student's school history and parent-teacher conferences. This chapter provides a detailed example how those keywords can guide our research for more effective ways of addressing academic and behavioral difficulties. During this exploration, we will use the following three guiding questions to investigate and identify proper methods of instruction and intervention.

Figure 17.1   Use Keywords to Research Interventions

Guiding Question 1: Specifically, what are your child's or student's difficulties?

Guiding Question 2: Why?

Guiding Question 3: What does research show to be an effective solution? In other words, what are the active ingredients?

Guiding Question 1: Specifically, what are your child or student's difficulties?

We can study the keywords we identified in Step 16. What are the top two or three areas that are causing the most pain for the student/instructor/parent? Then, describe what it looks and sounds like in the classroom and/or home. Be specific. Use books or the Internet to help you write detailed specifics.

Example

Vet's mother reviewed the keywords from her son's school history and parent-teacher conferences: difficulty learning to read, makes frequent reading errors, low reading fluency, and low reading comprehension. She found a few good websites that gave her more information, and she created the following chart. She was surprised at how much better she felt afterwards. She began to feel optimistic now that she more fully understood the *specific* difficulties her son was experiencing in the areas of reading.

Figure 17.2   Specific Difficulties Related to Reading

Poor Decoding Skills	Low Reading Fluency Rate	Poor Comprehension
He had difficulty learning to read. He still lacks accuracy while reading and/or makes frequent errors.	He reads slowly and it often sounds choppy with pauses.	He does not understand as he reads and/or does not remember what he has read afterwards.
Specifically,	Specifically,	Specifically,
He reads only prominent letters in a word and retrieves a similar word (word substitutions).	He doesn't recognize words he encounters while reading.	He can't keep track of what he's reading as he is reading.
He adds sounds that aren't in the word (sound additions).	He lacks reading accuracy and makes frequent errors and mistakes.	After reading a passage, he can't retain details from what he's read.
He deletes sounds of letters in the word he's reading (sound deletions).		
He says one sound when it's another (sound substitutions).		

Guiding Question 2: Why?

We can research, attend conferences, read articles, and watch videos to find the root causes of our child or teen's specific issues.

Example

As Vet's mother read articles about her child's difficulties, she also noted the reasons why each problem may occur. She added the following information to her chart.

Figure 17.3   Ask "Why?" to Find the Root Causes of Reading Difficulties

Poor Decoding Skills	Low Reading Fluency Rate	Poor Comprehension
Why?	Why?	Why?
He doesn't know the sounds of a lot of letters and letter groups (poor phonemic awareness).	He doesn't sound out words and when I ask him to, it's often inaccurate (poor decoding skills).	He can't remember what he's read because he is working so hard to figure out (decode) a word. Plus, he doesn't have enough working memory to keep track of what he's reading.
He doesn't really hear, distinguish, or identify individual sounds in words (lack of phonic knowledge).	He doesn't recognize a word he should know by now (poor sight word recognition).	He reads so slowly (fluency rate). Plus, he can't retain details from what he's read because he has poor short-term memory.
Struggles with sequencing of letters and sounds.	He doesn't have a strong vocabulary to pull from (limited lexicon).	

Guiding Question 3: What does research show to be an effective solution? In other words what are the "active ingredients?"

Siegrid Cooper, Speech Language Pathologist, adapted concepts of Warren, Fey, & Yoder (2007) to explain how parents can view the delivery of interventions in school settings (Cooper, 2014):

What is the "active ingredient" in the school's reading prescription? For example: Would you accept if your doctor told you he was going to prescribe your child a pill for an infection, but everyone knew the pill had only INERT INGREDIENTS, no ACTIVE INGREDIENTS? Schools must be asked, what is the "active ingredient" in what they are doing that will effect change? If they cannot provide you that answer, how will you know what needs to be changed if there is no improvement? Frequently the school will suggest changing the "form" of the pill (e.g., small group setting) or frequency (e.g., additional 30 minutes a day of intervention in tier 2 of RTI), but they NEVER want to discuss the ACTIVE INGREDIENT because that's about THEM (accountability). Being provided the "opportunity" is an inert ingredient.

While investigating solutions and "active ingredients" that have been shown to be effective, use reputable sources on the Internet such as research studies, university and gov websites, and books.

Example

Once Vet's mother listed her son's specific difficulties, then she was ready to search for the answers to the third guiding question: What does research show to be an effective solution? In other words, what are the "active ingredients?"

Vet's mom came across the following research regarding effective solutions:

Research supports that the following characteristics of instruction improve the reading proficiency of struggling readers: (1) explicitly and systematically introducing and teaching that letters and letter groups represent sounds, (2) combining phonemic awareness and phonics (3) using a multisensory approach to help students build the sound-symbol relationship in a memorable way, (4) providing practice reading the sequence of letters, letter groups, and syllables in words using blending strategies, and (5) handwriting and spelling exercises that mirror the student's instruction in phonics.

- **Systematically Introduce Letters, Letter Groups, and Syllables**
Phonemes are the smallest units of speech. A letter between slashes like /f/ represents the sound *f* makes in the word *fish*. Phonics is how letters and letter groups represent the sounds of spoken language. It involves hearing a sound with the letter or letter group. For example, the letter *a* can make the *short a* sound in *apple*, the *long a* sound in *baby*, the *short o* sound in *spa*, and the *short u* sound in *panda*. The letter groups *au, aw, and al* can make *short o* sound in *laundry, straw, and chalk* (Hunter, 2013). This illustrates how English can be confusing and explains why some instructors are reluctant to teach it.

The importance of providing phonics instruction that is explicit and systematic has been widely documented. When phonics is taught explicitly, it means the instructor clearly explains the rules (patterns) of phonics and that nothing is implied. When phonics is taught systematically, instruction and blending of letters, letter groups, and syllables are organized and introduced to the student in a logical sequence based on the sounds. For example, consonant sounds are introduced first. Next, students learn primary short vowel sounds (a, e, i, o, u), followed by long vowel sounds (CV, vowel teams, VCV). Afterwards, students are introduced to advanced long and short vowel spelling patterns and other vowel sounds (ou, ow, oi, oy, oo, r-controlled). Lastly, syllables are introduced in a similar order (Hunter, 2013). Without sequential instruction and practice, it is extremely difficult for many children to develop their decoding skills.

- **Combine Phonemic Awareness Instruction with Spelling Instruction**

Phonemic awareness is the ability to hear, identify, and manipulate the **individual** sounds. For example, do you hear the /i/ sound in the words *igloo, sit, insect, and thin*? (yes). And how many /e/ sounds do you hear in the word *pepper*? (one). Students can practice identifying phonemes in listening exercises. Also, teachers can model how to break down and segment words sound by sound to spell words. Say the word *sharp* slowly, so you can hear each sound. (/sh/ /ar/ /p/)

The National Reading Panel issued a report in 2000 titled *Teaching Children to Read* in response to a mandate by Congress. The panel reviewed 100,000 studies examining the effectiveness of reading instruction for struggling readers in kindergarten through third grade. Their findings showed that teaching phonemic awareness helps all children learn how to read and spell. Specifically, teaching students how to convert letters and letter groups into sounds and blending the sounds to create recognizable words improves reading skills. In addition, teaching students how to convert words into letters and letter groups to segment the words improves spelling. Combining phonemic awareness training with instruction in letter-sound knowledge provides greater benefits than by providing phonemic awareness training alone (Eunice Kennedy Shriver NICHHD, 2001, p 5).

Phonological awareness is a bigger umbrella. Phonological awareness is the ability to hear, identify, and manipulate **individual sounds, parts of words, and syllables.** For example, what words rhyme with *stand? (hand, land, sand)*. And how many syllables are in the words *discuss, chicken,* and *exhale*? (2) And how do you segment them into syllables? (*dis-cuss, chick-en, ex-hale*). And what syllable pattern can you hear in the words *si-lent* and *tri-umph*? (The first syllable ends with a *long i* sound). Practice segmenting multisyllable words into syllables trains students to read and spell manageable chunks.

- **Use Multisensory Techniques and Memory Strategies**

Rote memorization is particularly difficult for students with dyslexia, ADHD, and orthographic processing deficits. It does not mean people with poor rote memory have a poor memory altogether. They can have an excellent memory of *experiences* and for information that has *meaning and purpose* attached to it. However, rote learning is learning through memorization. Some examples of things you may have learned by rote include memorizing the ABC song, months of the year, state capitols, and multiplication tables (4 x 6 = 24).

Because readers with dyslexia, ADHD, and orthographic processing deficits have difficulty learning information by rote, they have an especially difficult time learning and memorizing letters and their sounds. That is why it is important for them to learn the letters, letter groups, and their sounds in a way that they will remember.

Research supports and substantiates the need for multisensory phonics. Multisensory means using multiple senses (sight, sound, touch, etc.) to help a person memorize something. We can use multisensory techniques during handwriting, speaking, and listening exercises. For example, a multisensory technique we commonly use to memorize words for a spelling test would be to write (touch) the word while sounding it out (sound) *as* it is written. Students build the sound-symbol relationship in spelling exercises when they simultaneously say individual sounds while writing each corresponding letter or letter group. You can also use 3-dimensional visual images, colors, textures, light, and conjure feelings to create lasting impressions. Students can create color-coded 3-D flash cards to anchor the letters and letter groups to their sounds (Hunter, 2013). This improves their ability to retrieve the sounds of letters and letter groups while reading. These same flash cards can also help students to map sounds to letters/letter groups when spelling (ibid).

Multisensory approaches use visual, auditory, kinesthetic, and tactile senses during reading, spelling, and writing instruction. Gillingham and Stillman created a multisensory program based on the work of Samuel T. Orton in the 1930's to remediate students' difficulties in reading, spelling, and handwriting. The Orton-Gillingham approach teaches the letters, letter groups, and their sounds whereby the student sees a letter (visual), says and hears its sound (auditory), and writes it (kinesthetic). Many current reading programs use Orton-Gillingham-based approaches.

· **Provide Practice Blending Letters, Letter Groups, and Syllables**
It is not enough to simply teach phonics. New readers and older students with low fluency rate should also be taught strategies for blending. Teachers and parents can teach blending. For example, to blend the word *peach*, ask the student to say the initial sound /p/ and the medial sound /ea/, then ask the student to combine them /pea/. Have the student repeat /pea/ and then add the final sound /ch/ to produce the entire word /peach/.

· **Handwriting and Spelling Exercises that Mirror Phonic Patterns**
Words that students read in stories must mirror and be linked to handwritten spelling activities that follow sound patterns.

This is missing from the vast majority of reading interventions. That is why numerous students who receive interventions for reading may become good readers, but never overcome their challenges in writing and spelling.

When students are in overload, their writing seems to greatly decrease in maturity; they do not use, or incorrectly use, skills which appeared to have been learned…Students with dyslexia or dysgraphia are in a predicament because they lack automaticity with lower level skills, such as letter formation, directionality, sound-symbol relationships, and early spelling patterns. This lack of automaticity almost ensures cognitive and attentional overload within the writing process. Such students are frequently able to verbally tell a story at a much higher level than they can write a similar story.

Excerpt from p. 37 of The Source for Dyslexia and Dysgraphia by Regina G. R ichards,, Austin, TX: PRO-ED, Inc. ©1999. Reprinted with permission. No further duplication allowed..

Students must practice identifying and recognizing phonic spelling patterns and mapping the sounds to letters and letter groups in writing exercises to increase the students' knowledge of orthographic spelling patterns in the words. So, it is critical to provide students with practice handwriting and spelling during their reading instruction. When students struggle with lower level skills such as handwriting and/or spelling. it is very difficult for them to work on more advanced skills in their written expression. Asking them to perfect higher-level tasks is like asking someone to perfect their swimming strokes when they are struggling just to stay above the water. However, after students practice the fundamentals, then we can demand that they master more advanced skills in written expression.

Handwritten spelling activities must include syllable spelling patterns, so that children can become better readers, writers, and spellers. Students will become more confident spellers and readers when they can accurately retrieve the letters, letter groups, and syllables that correspond to the sounds in the words they write.

Multiple exposures to different words using the same spelling patterns help students begin to identify patterns in the sounds and spellings of the English language. A systematic and cumulative approach introduces phonic spelling patterns based on the sounds. This will increase the students' phonemic and phonological awareness to increase phonic mapping and decoding abilities, which can increase reading fluency rate and comprehension.

During her research, Vet's mother created the following chart of solutions and active ingredients.

Figure 17.4   Find the Most Effective Solutions for Reading Difficulties

Poor Decoding Skills	Low Reading Fluency Rate	Poor Comprehension
Teach the letters, letter groups, and syllables with their sounds in a specific, organized manner that is clear to the learner (systematic and explicit, synthetic phonics instruction). Handwriting and spelling exercises that teach students to convert sounds into letters, letter groups, and syllables in a specific, organized manner that is clear to the learner (systematic and explicit spelling instruction). Teach blending strategies and provide practice blending letters, letter groups, and syllables.	Repeatedly expose students to sets of words in different activities over time to increase the speed they recognize the words (automaticity). Student rereads the same passage until the student can read it at an improved rate and with fewer errors (fluency building).	Teach students comprehension strategies to find the main idea of every paragraph. Practice decoding + working memory exercises. Practice fluency + short term memory exercises.

Instructors and parents of students with ADHD, dyslexia, dysgraphia, and autism (who are not proficient readers, writers, or spellers), it is essential to your students' success that you are familiar with the concepts in Step 15 and 16.

Lesson 17 | Researching Interventions

 Instructor or parent can complete this activity to help find the root causes for their child or student's difficulties.

Reread what you wrote for Journal 16 Getting to the Root Cause.

Answer the three guiding questions to research interventions and methods of effective instruction.

Guiding Question 1: Specifically, what are your child's or student's difficulties?
Guiding Question 2: Why?

Guiding Question 3: What does research show to be an effective solution? What are the active ingredients?

Create a chart with the answers to the three guiding questions to link your child's or student's difficulties with solutions (and active ingredients).

Journal 17 | Supplying Intervention

 Instructor or parent journals:

Reflect on who and how you may share this information. Whose attention, energy, and conscious actions are needed to help your child or student improve?

Prepare a report using the information from the chart you created in Lesson 17 Researching Interventions.

STEP 18 | **HONOR THEIR DIFFERENCES**

ACKNOWLEDGE AND ACCEPT THAT THEY ARE DIFFERENT

Scenario 1: A teacher laments, "My curriculum and methods work for 80% of my students, they should work for the other 20%. Why can't these kids just learn? They know what they are supposed to do. I tell them over and over. They just won't do it. They just don't care and have poor work ethics."

Scenario 2: Another teacher asserts, "It's a brand new year and a couple of my students are already back-talking me and won't do their work. They just find ways to get into trouble."

Scenario 3: A parent expresses, "I don't know what's wrong with my son. I have another son and daughter, older than he is and they turned out just fine. School wasn't a problem for them. But, he won't do the work, and he gets into trouble. He is so stubborn and hard-headed. I've raised him the same as my other two. I don't know what's wrong."

You may relate to one of these scenarios and wonder if your child or student(s) will ever be able to learn. You may believe that you will never gain the respect and cooperation from them. Dear reader, the winds can shift direction, and so can the behavior and work ethic of a child.

I have had the blessing of working with some of these "willful" and "stubborn" children, and I firmly believe all young children begin wanting to please their teachers and parents. However at some point, they experience intense difficulty developing skills in some area: academic, behavioral or emotional. Many "hard-headed" students suffer from weaknesses with rote memory, short-term memory, sequencing of multiple steps, reading social cues, cultural/linguistic differences, etc. Their tribulations frustrate them, and they avoid, escape, or act out in ways that make them appear as though they are willful and not self-disciplined.

As teachers, tutors, coaches, and parents, we can teach these children, and we can gain respect and cooperation from our most problematic youngsters. How? For me, I had to first understand that God did not make us all on an assembly line. When my students couldn't do what I was asking, I had to remind myself that we were not shaped and formed with cookie cutters and each brain works differently. I had to realize these differences are what make our Earth turn. We need individuals with different skills, abilities, communication styles, preferences, dispositions, and ways of thinking to make our workplaces and communities prosper. Even though someone else's brain was not like mine, I had to accept it and understand what to do, so I could teach them. More importantly, I stopped judging, because I didn't know what kind of difference they would make later in life. It helped me to keep in mind that some of the most successful people have experienced and overcame some of the same weaknesses that were driving me crazy. By acknowledging and accepting their differences, I could teach them how to overcome their obstacles and help them succeed.

USE THE INDIVIDUALITY QUESTIONNAIRE

Teachers and parents can use the Individuality Questionnaire to understand the characteristics that make each child an individual. You may not know the answers to every question. That's okay. Answer as many of the question as you can, and it will help you develop a vision that will lead you and your student to success.

Figure 18.1   Individuality Questionnaire

Perceptual style? (visual, auditory, tactual, kinesthetic)

Disposition? (global, analytical)

Multiple intelligence? (verbal-linguistic, logical-mathematical, visual-spatial, musical-rhythmic, interpersonal, intrapersonal, and/or naturalist)

Metacognitive processes?

Dyslexia, Dysgraphia, ADHD, Autism, OCD, English Learner, Gifted & Talented?

504/IEP?

Knowledge base, skills, strategies, strengths, weaknesses?

Specific behaviors? (academic, social, emotional, physical)

Reason for misbehaviors? (attention, power, revenge, avoidance of failure)

Antecedents? (does not understand or process directions, proximity to others, transitions, frustrated, uninterested, bored, distracted, tactile, etc.)

How does this student respond to different types of consequences?

Reinforcements/forms of praise? (active listening, show interest, encourage, care for class pet, stand near, sit beside, smile, nod, thumbs up, pat on back, high five, computer time, positive note home to parent, bingo cards, private compliment)

Cultural characteristics and considerations?

How could I collaborate, train, engage, and empower parents/family?

Who could this student support?

How could this student contribute to his/her peers, family, school, or community?

What could this student do to feel more empowered?

What boundaries and expectations does this student need?

How could this student be more constructive? Productive?

How could this student learn the value of a good education?

How could this student become more committed to learning?

How could this student develop strong guiding values? Social competencies? A positive identity?

How could I best support this student?

How could the family best support this student?

Who else could provide additional support and in what way?

DIFFERENTIATE YOUR INSTRUCTION

The next step towards academic, behavioral, and emotional success is attempting to honor your child's or students' differences by differentiating your instruction through activities, curriculum, materials, intervention programs, techniques, supports, and/or guidance. Differentiated instruction follows the notion that students are not alike in how they learn.

It is not easy to teach a classroom of students with different learning styles, levels of abilities, dispositions, communication styles, and the list goes on. Teaching and parenting become easier and more effective when we acknowledge people's differences and address each person as an individual. Some of the valuable byproducts include: improved learning, respect, cooperation, and a significant decrease in undesirable behaviors in the classroom and at home.

We tend to dismiss what we do not know. In other words, if we are not familiar with something or it seems nebulous to us, we may gloss over it or skip it altogether. Differentiating instruction should not be one of those things. Please give it a try. I boiled down what could be an overwhelming amount of information into a comprehensive and concise lesson for teachers, tutors, and coaches. Parents, you will also benefit from studying this, so you may learn how to differentiate instruction when helping your child with homework, homeschooling, or providing intervention.

USE THE DIFFERENTIATING INSTRUCTION CHECKLIST

Parents, you have had years of experience working with your children in a variety of ways. You've observed them doing their homework, participating in school activities, and you've seen how they've responded to different teachers and teaching styles. You have a decent understanding of their characteristics and needs. As you read through this step, you can gain an even better understanding. Use this information to communicate with your children's teachers and advocate for them to receive instruction and strategies that will honor their differences and help them become more successful in school.

Teachers, if differentiating instruction is new to you, then begin trying it out with one or two students. You can refer to Figure 18 Differentiating Instruction Checklist as a guide. Teachers, especially, can use it to innovate their curriculum, materials, activities, and interventions during each stage of the instruction cycle. Don't feel as if you have to understand and do everything on the list! Study the choices and check off the areas you think your student(s) would benefit from receiving. Frequently, refer to it to insure your instruction is learner-centered, thematic, interactive, and assessment-driven. It will assist you in designing lessons, so students will connect to what they are learning and, hence, remember newly learned information for homework, tests, and reports. Do not hesitate to collaborate and partner with teachers and parents.

Figure 18.2 Differentiating Instruction Checklist

Pre-Assess

__ Use formal or informal (questioning) to pre-assess skills and knowledge.
__ Document data using rubrics, t-charts, or checklists.
__ Study data and let my students' needs drive instruction.
__ Study benchmarks and other assessments to determine my target students.

Plan the Lesson

__ Match learning objectives to activities for students with different perceptual styles, dispositions, and multiple intelligences.
__ Plan sequence, demonstrations, visuals, and gather materials.
__ Review students' cultural quizzes and integrate students' interests, backgrounds, and experiences into your lesson.

Introduce the Lesson

__ Get students' attention (visual, auditory, kinesthetic, and tactile)
__ State objectives and expectations to students
__ Direct teach using systematic instruction that introduces information in sequential order
__ Model processes and explain what I was thinking during each step
__ Explicitly teach vocabulary, concept, or process
__ Check for understanding, make modifications, and differentiate
__ Vary my pace of instruction to a swift pace
__ Activate students' background knowledge
__ Have students make Connections, Wonderings, and Observations
__ Make lessons Visual, Auditory, Kinesthetic, Tactile (VAKT)
__ Identify and distinguish differences with highlighting, color markers, color-coding, boxing keywords, and folding notepaper
__ Use examples, non-examples, and mnemonics
__ Concrete vs. abstract

Guided Practice

__ Model procedures and what's expected
__ Proximity, circulation, and questioning are critical to monitor comprehension and provide corrective feedback
__ Give students rubrics, t-charts, or checklists, if needed
__ Check for understanding (assess) and then clarify, model, provide immediate corrective feedback, make modifications, & differentiate
__ Increase student engagement
__ Question so students can actively respond; increase opportunities to respond
__ Vary pace of instruction to a swift pace
__ Identify and distinguish differences with highlighting, color markers, color-coding, boxing keywords, and folding notepaper
__ Activate students' background knowledge to interest students, maintain attention, and increase student engagement

Activity or Independent Practice

__ Students may work individually, in pairs, or in small groups
__ Provide opportunity in class practice to increase students' recall
__ Proximity, circulation, and questioning are critical to monitor comprehension and provide corrective feedback
__ Assess and provide feedback and an opportunity for students to make corrections
__ Give students rubrics, t-Charts, or checklists, if needed
__ Provide opportunities for application, synthesis, and abstract thinking
__ Flash cards

Make Adjustments

__ Reflect, evaluate, and make changes to lesson for the next time

Spiral Curriculum

__ Provide multiple exposures to concepts to review previously mentioned concepts, vocabulary, and processes
__ Provide multiple opportunities for students to practice skills and increase recall

Post-Assess

__ Compare progress with initial benchmark data
__ Document data using a rubric, t-chart, or checklist
__ Evaluate if objectives/expectations were met
__ Study data and let my students' needs drive instruction
__ Study benchmarks and other assessments to determine my target students

Throughout the Lesson Plan & Instruction Cycle

__ Increase target students' feelings of success
__ Provide positive reinforcement (be swift, specific, sincere)
__ Link positive results to the actions of the student
__ Provide encouragement
__ Provide scaffolding, prompts, or cues
__ Provide purpose, meaning, and relevance

DECIDE WHICH AREA(S) YOU WANT TO ASSESS

We must measure the student's performance in the areas we want them to achieve. Think of how you can evaluate the effectiveness of your instruction, curriculum, materials, or interventions.

How could you measure and monitor the child's progress over time?

What do you want to improve? What does good reading, writing, etc. look like? Ask yourself, "What is the desired outcome? What skills are needed to make that happen? How could you measure it?"

Figure 18.3   Areas We Can Assess and Measure

Reading	**Oral Reading Fluency** how many correct words the student can read per minute
Math	**Computational Fluency** how many correct addition, subtraction, multiplication, division, or fraction equivalents are computed per minute
Spelling	**Orthographic Spelling Patterns** how many spelling patterns are written correctly
Writing	**Writing Samples** how many elements of handwriting and/or written expression are used and improve over the school year
Behavior	**Inappropriate behavior** how many times the student behaves inappropriately in a specified timeframe (e.g. 15 minutes, 30 minutes) during a class over a specific time period (e.g. one month, a grading period)

DESIGN YOUR ASSESSMENT

There are a variety of assessments. Some assessments help teachers identify students' characteristics, strengths, and weaknesses. Some help teachers, parents, and students compare where a student falls in comparison with other students. Others can monitor students' progress and growth in specific areas.

A good coach frequently assesses athletes' skills and studies videos of their players and their performance. Afterwards, they offer constructive feedback so players can make adjustments. Similarly, instructors should design assessments to evaluate the performance of our students and offer constructive feedback like a good coach.

Figure 18.4   We Assess so We Can Give Feedback and Make Adjustments

Teachers and parents can design simple assessments that visually provide feedback on how the learner is doing to increase awareness and help everyone make adjustments. You can create assessments that use visuals, instead of words, to motivate and help students learn. They can be created to assess almost any skill or behavior you would like to improve (e.g. content knowledge, listening skills, tasks, responsibilities, teamwork).

Some of the most effective assessments are simple and involve the child. Here's one example of a fun assessment that involves the child. A student is shown a map of the continents (or planets) and given seven (or 9) alien figurines. The student gets to physically place an alien figurine on a continent (or planet) after each sentence they write (or math problem is solved). Try to think of ways you can design informal assessments that motivate and help children and teens learn, as well as provide data.

MONITOR PROGRESS

Progress monitoring allows teachers and parents to see if what they are doing is making a difference. Tracking a learner's growth over time allows teachers, parents, and/or administrators to see the impact instructional activities, curriculum, materials, interventions, and classroom/home variables has on performance. That way, if a child does not make enough progress, then the teacher can make adjustments and differentiate instruction. In this way we can more effectively take actions in the areas needing improvement. If we see no improvements, then that is your cue to refer to Figure 18.2 Differentiating Instruction Checklist for more ideas.

ASSESS BEHAVIOR SKILLS

Teachers and parents can provide students with natural remedies to help children improve their behaviors. First, we have to identify the behavior we want to improve. Then we can study and document their behavior to determine what exactly are they doing, when, and for how long.

We can use functional behavior assessments for collecting data for all kinds of problem behaviors. Do you want to find out if eating certain foods or lack of sleep really affects your child's behaviors? Or want to find out why "random" outbursts are occurring? Or what effect transitions have on a child? Or is something you're doing or not doing making a difference? Track it. Parents and teachers can use functional behavioral assessments to track behaviors and the things that may trigger and affect behavior. Once we look for patterns and gather reasons and influences, we can try new ideas (develop a behavioral intervention plan) and differentiate instruction, activities, materials, etc.

Functional Behavioral Assessment & Positive Behavioral Intervention and Support

- Identify the behavior (specific, observable, and measurable).
- Identify when the student is most likely and least likely to engage in the behavior.
- Identify triggers (stimulus that sparks the behavior).
- Identify setting events (events that occurred before).
- Conduct behavioral recording by documenting the frequency and duration of the behavior(s) over time (every 15 minutes, 30 minutes, class period, day, or week)
- Graph assessment data.
- Analyze, look for patterns, and develop a hypothesis. Include each behavior's function, factors, environment variables, social interactions, and influences.
- Conduct experiments to verify or revise hypothesis.
- Develop a behavioral intervention plan.
- Set goals; describe intervention, prescribed teacher responses, replacement behaviors.
- Teach alternative behaviors and modify circumstances.
- Recognize and praise student's efforts. State your belief in their potential.
- Note changes, evaluate, and modify curriculum, instruction activities, materials, or interventions.
- Point out progress over time to student.

It's commonly thought that if only students would behave, then students could learn and there would be no academic failure. However, as you've learned in previous steps, students can disguise their frustration or anxiety of academic weaknesses and failures. Futhermore, students with academic weaknesses also shift their teachers' focus away from their inabilities by goofing off, acting out, escape tactics, or rebelling. However, if we can address students' difficulties then their frustrations will no longer manifest themselves in inappropriate conduct, which will save us time and frustration. But more importantly, we will earn our student's respect and make a significant and lasting difference in our children and teen's lives.

We should ask, "*What academic weaknesses exist; and, could they be the root cause of their undesirable behaviors?*" If not, then we can begin speculating whether the student struggles with (monitoring and managing) his or her social and emotional behaviors.

UNDERSTAND HOW THEY REMEMBER NEWLY LEARNED INFORMATION

Every student in a classroom does not learn the same way. Students with strong auditory skills learn wll by hearing what the teacher says. Students who do not have strong auditory skills may have difficulties remembering what is said. We can help those students comprehend and remember what we're teaching by showing graphics, 3-D objects, video clips, demonstrations, highlighting, and color-coding during your lectures.

PROVIDE INTERACTIVE INSTRUCTION THAT GIVES STUDENTS OPPORTUNITIES TO RESPOND

There are many benefits of teaching one-to-one and small group settings. That is why a parent is an ideal teacher. If a parent cannot make the time or does not have the patience, consider providing a tutor.

In school settings, one-to-one and small group instruction can be effective because students are given opportunities to interact with the instructor, ask questions, discuss meanings of words, receive valuable corrective feedback, confirm their knowledge, and thus gain confidence. If teachers do not have the ability to teach one-to-one or in a small group setting, they can still provide interactive instruction.

It's unrealistic to think students can just sit quietly and listen to us teach a lesson and memorize everything. Providing frequent interaction during instruction is one of the most significant ways a teacher or tutor can differentiate instruction for underperforming students, English language learners, and students with behavioral challenges. Keeping students engaged with interactive questions and dialogue fosters academic and behavioral successes.

All students, especially shy ones, would benefit from interaction using white boards. For example, after teaching a concept, such as writing an algebraic equation in slope-intercept form, you could check for their understanding using white boards. First, project an equation to the class.
$9 + y = 3x$

Then, ask students to re-write the equation in slope-intercept form.
$y = 3x - 9$

Monitor the students' behaviors. Are they uncertain or confident? Who looks at someone else's answer? Don't call anyone out. Just try to explain it again and then give everyone another chance.

Also, increase student engagement and teach different learning styles by offering a variety of student activities. Allow students to demonstrate their knowledge in a variety of ways. Here are some ideas.

- Skits, oral presentations, role-play
- Movies, video clips, project images from the computer
- Music, create songs
- Cartoons, posters, murals, coloring book
- Scrapbook, PowerPoint presentations, create websites
- Diorama, make models, 3-D objects
- Themed games, puzzles
- Demonstrations, labs
- Journal
- Interview
- News report, commentary
- Discussions, dialogue
- Describe patterns
- Outlines, timelines
- 3-D flash cards
- Maps, globes
- Word search, I Spy
- Field trips

PROVIDE INTERACTION AND DIALOGUE THAT IS CULTURALLY RESPONSIVE

Culturally responsive teaching was introduced in Step 15 Be Relevant. Integrating students' interests and cultures into their assignments and activities adds interest to their assignments. Their classwork becomes relevant and motivates them. Being culturally responsive can help us differentiate instruction and improve interaction, dialogue, and assignments to increase student engagement. Responding to different communication styles, dispositions, backgrounds, and experiences is the essence of differentiating instruction and addressing students' needs. Students need to recognize themselves in the curriculum and in the work we are asking them to do. They need to be noticed and cared for. When we show that we respect and care about them, they will be more willing to show their respect and care for us.

Often times, culturally sensitive issues may come up and students may ask difficult questions. Teachers can respect families and cultural differences by responding, "Some topics are best discussed within the family and my opinion may differ." Or, "Let me tell you what it means to me. But, remember, I am one person and others may feel differently."

Lesson 18 | Individuality Questionnaire and Differentiating Instruction

 Faculty or parent can observe your child or student(s) in the classroom using a functional behavioral assessment described in Step 18. Then complete the following activity.

Before observing a student in the classroom, review any school history, documentation (such as IEP's, 504 Accommodations, report cards), notes from home, teachers, etc. Next, use Figure 18.1 Individuality Questionnaire at the beginning of this step to help you answer the questions and find your student's unique blend of characteristics.

After observing the student, review Figure 18.2 Differentiating Instruction Checklist and check off how you or the teacher(s) will differentiate instruction.

Journal 18 | Design Your Assessments

 Faculty, instructor or parent journals:

Decide the desired behaviors you would like to see in your child or student. Determine what skill(s) the student would need to improve. This will determine what you will assess. Then, design your assessments.

Assess your student(s) and monitor progress.

Think of yourself as a coach. How will you offer corrective feedback to your student(s)? After each assessment, ask yourself the following questions:

- Were any of my assumptions wrong?
- Where do I need to make course-corrections?
- Should I modify my assessments to gain more accurate information?
- What adjustments do I need to make related to my materials, curriculum, activities, interventions, methods, personnel, or instruction?

This journal activity is not just for teachers. Tutors, coaches, principals, parents, anyone can assess any skill, design informal assessments, and monitor progress. It's not rocket science; it's using the scientific method. If 8th grade students can use the scientific method during their science fair projects, so can anyone else who wants to become more aware and conscientious to solve problems. Knowledge is power, but solving problems is even more powerful, because it leads to empowerment.

STEP 19 | DESIGN A SCHOOL-WIDE INTERVENTION

DECIDE IF A SCHOOL-WIDE INTERVENTION IS NECESSARY

It may seem as though student behaviors, such as bullying, violence, promiscuity, or depression, are widespread in some schools. When this happens, it may become necessary for school principals or administrators to uncover and address the root causes.

Likewise, school principals or administrators may also want to address the root causes for significant differences in their students' grades, test scores, and achievement gaps.

We can't correct behaviors and achievement gaps overnight. It will take more than teachers supplying academic or behavioral interventions. It is a process that requires focus on more than one level or tier. And, school personnel can achieve better results in a faster time frame with the combined efforts of teachers, students, their families, administrators, and the community.

CONSIDER USING A 3-TIERED APPROACH "CAFETERIA" STYLE

By using a "cafeteria" style approach, school administrators and staff can custom-design 3 tiers of prevention and intervention. You can pick and choose what is right for your unique student body and faculty, based on the results you would like to achieve. Think about your students and the results you would like to achieve. What would you like to improve? Achievement gaps? Test scores and outcomes for students with math, reading, spelling, and writing difficulties? Outcomes for students from cultural and linguistic backgrounds? Behaviors such as bullying, depression, anxiety, and physical fitness? Social and/or educational equality?

Figure 19.1   Three-Tiered Approach for School-Wide Interventions

	Identify specific problems or areas you want to improve. Determine what data will be collected and tracked, who you will assess, and what assessments you will use.
Tier 1	Develop a plan for how your school will use preventative approaches to address the problem or area you want to improve in **general education classroom settings for all students.**
Tier 2	Develop a plan for how your school will address the problem **for target students needing intervention inside and/or outside of the general classroom.**
Tier 3	Develop a plan for how your school will address the needs of the most challenging students to receive the most intensive interventions in **small group or one-to-one settings.**
	Monitor the progress of the students in the areas of achievement.

After you've identified specific problems or the areas you would like to improve, consider what could be done on different levels or tiers.

Tier 1 interventions address the **general population of students**. How? On this level, teachers and staff members provide *preventative* approaches to *all* students within general education classrooms, gyms, hallways, restrooms, cafeterias, and playgrounds.

Tier 2 interventions address **specific students** inside and/or outside of the classrooms. These specific individuals could receive tier 2 interventions in a variety of ways: differentiated classroom instruction, curriculum, programs, training, supports, guidance, counseling, and/or mentoring.

Tier 3 interventions address the needs of the **students who are most affected**. They should receive the most intensive interventions in small group or one-to-one settings. Right now, don't think about how all of this will be accomplished and who exactly would be able to do it. For now, just try to envision some possible solutions for each of the three tiers.

Lastly, think about what data should be collected and tracked. What assessments could be used, and who would be responsible for the assessments? Consider the various ways the students and staff's progress can be measured and monitored.

The idea of implementing a school-wide intervention can make a teacher, principal, or superintendent feel overwhelmed or defeated before they even begin. You may be thinking, "We are already spread too thin. We just don't have time to work with our students more than we already are." However, school-wide interventions are not about making teachers work more. It's about solving problems that are draining everyone's time, energy, and motivation. If we don't solve these draining problems, our schools can become unpleasant places to work that substantially decrease our quality of life.

During the remainder of this unit, you'll read how an example school implemented a school-wide intervention. As the story unfolds, I hope you will be able to imagine how you can address areas and improve your school's culture and climate.

IDENTIFY THE SPECIFIC AREAS YOU WANT TO ADDRESS IN YOUR SCHOOL

Designing a "cafeteria" style intervention begins with identifying specific problems or areas you want to improve school-wide. Look to data to find which students are having the most difficulties and identify their student characteristics. For more information on student characteristics, refer to Figure 18.1 Individuality Checklist in Step 18 Honor Their Differences.

Example

Here's how an example school designed an intervention "cafeteria" style. The hypothetical name of the school is Austin Middle School. Consistently over the past few years, the student body has been around 30% White, 10% Black, 54% Hispanic, 3% Asian, 2% Native American/Alaska Native, and 1% Native Hawaiian/Pacific Islander. The administration noticed over the years there has been an achievement gap between their White and Black students. On the last state mandated tests, 9% of their White students scored below "basic" on the Reading portion of the test. In comparison, 45% of their Black students scored below "basic" on the Reading portion of the test. They also have noticed that their Black students had a significantly high number of school suspensions, in-school suspensions, and referrals to the office. The administrators identified that the two areas they wanted to address were academic achievement and discipline rates for their African American students.

At the next staff meeting, the administrators of Austin Middle School reported the results from the most recent state mandated test scores. The principal announced that their efforts in trying to close the achievement gaps for their African-American students had been unsuccessful again. He followed by saying he would take full responsibility for the failure and hoped that everyone would be on board with the adjustments that would need to be made.

He thanked the staff and said, "The intervention we were using this year, and last, improved the test scores of our White students, but not our African American students. We must figure out how we can narrow the gap." The principal added, "Research shows interventions that work with one culture or learning style may not produce the same results in students from another culture or learning style. I think we proved that." He continued, "It's time we not only scrutinize our instruction, but also our systems, rules, and practices that may be contributing to the educational inequalities. We need to prepare to make some serious adjustments. It's time. Let's think outside of the 'White' box. I hope you will join me in making some cross-cultural changes."

SHARE YOUR GOALS WITH POTENTIAL SOURCES OF SUPPORT

Identify specific problems you want to address most. Then, link each problem to a goal and think of who could help your school reach those goals.

Example

The staff sat quietly and listened in despair. One of the teachers raised his hand and said he didn't know how he would be able to fit another thing into his day. The principal responded, "Addressing social and educational inequalities will not be easy. But we really don't have a choice, and we have to find a way because it's the right thing to do. And, we will not have to do it alone." He shared the goals in Figure 19.2 with the staff and followed each goal with potential sources of support.

Figure 19.2   Goals with Potential Sources of Support

Improve School Culture	Increase Teacher Success	Increase Parent Involvement and Support	Increase Student Success in Reading and Decrease Discipline Rates
Administration	Teachers	Parent Teacher Association (PTA)	Volunteer Tutors
Faculty	Counselors	Parent Support Specialist	University Staff and Students
Staff	Coaches	Students' Families	Community Organizations
Instructional Coordinators	Principal		Business Leaders
School District Personnel	Instructional Specialists		Parent Teacher Association (PTA)
Parent Teacher Association (PTA)	School District Personnel		
	Parent Teacher Association (PTA)		

DECIDE WHAT YOU WILL DO IN THE GENERAL CLASSROOMS (TIER 1)

After you have identified goals, think about how you can achieve them in general education classrooms, hallways, restrooms, gyms, cafeterias, and playgrounds. Think about what could be done for all students. What is needed of teachers and staff? What kind of instruction, approaches, materials, and techniques could improve the specific areas you want to address in all classrooms? Look to research and studies. What have other schools tried?

Example

Two assistant principals took the floor. They began by sharing the research on preventative instruction and approaches that could address low achievement and high discipline rates for all African American students in their general education classroom settings. One of the assistant principals asked, "What changes can we make in our classrooms, hallways, restrooms, gyms, cafeteria, and playgrounds that will promote making better grades and scholarly attitudes?" He answered his own question by saying, "Referring students to the office and in-school suspensions are not motivating our students to make better grades or improving their attitudes. When we send them out of the classroom, they miss valuable classroom instruction and it puts them further behind. This does not cultivate a scholarly attitude."

The assistant principal recommended that their school use the following study as an example to follow. It was a multi-school pilot project that was designed to close achievement gaps for African American students. It was conducted by AEL (Appalachia Educational Laboratory) and the purpose of the project was to determine if professional development and culturally responsive instruction and materials would produce improved teacher and student behaviors and raise the academic achievement of all students, specifically their African American students. Two elementary, one middle school, and one high school participated in the study. Each Pilot School had at least 25% African American population. Four schools that received no treatment served as a comparison.

He explained that culturally responsive teaching research-based principles includes providing positive culturally or linguistically diverse perspectives, cultural sensitivity, and reshaping the curriculum to include positive contributions of cultures other than European American (Hughes, 2005). He emphatically stressed, "We must use instructional materials that present both minority and majority perspectives. That way our students can imagine themselves in what they are reading. Teachers should strive to find curriculum and books that include some of the language, norms, and cultures that our students can relate to."

The assistant principal ended by noting that The AEL study found that "Participants in the Pilot Schools intervention showed growth over time in their understanding of (1) the impact of culture and ethnicity on teaching and learning in classrooms and (2) the value of culturally relevant instruction in narrowing the achievement gap" (Hughes, 2005, p 52). The interventions used in the AEL study had also made an impact on teachers. Teachers felt they had created "a culturally responsive learning environment (e.g., using culturally mediated instruction, using multiracial materials, encouraging student-controlled classroom discourse)" and concluded, "respecting students' cultures is important for teaching African American students" (Hughes, 2005, p 52).

Austin Middle School staff decided that their tier 1 intervention for their general education classrooms would require professional development that includes topics similar to the ones covered in Step 15 Be Relevant. The culturally responsive faculty training would include a cultural self-assessment, an analysis of biases, paradigm shifts, and reshaping the curriculum.

DECIDE INTERVENTIONS FOR YOUR TARGET STUDENTS (TIER 2)

Tier 1 interventions are preventative approaches that address the problem or area your school would like to improve in the general classrooms. Remember tier 1 addresses all students and teachers, whereas tier 2 targets specific students and teachers. When developing a plan for your tier 2 interventions, look to your data to decide which students will be targeted, what intervention(s) will be provided, who will provide it, and when and where they will take place. Also, consider what is needed of teachers and staff. Research a variety of instruction, approaches, materials, curriculum, and techniques that could improve the specific areas you want to address. Examine different studies and actions other schools have tried.

Example

One of the two Austin Middle School counselors took the floor to make recommendations for tier 2 interventions. He suggested providing reading interventions to the African American students who did not pass Reading benchmark tests. They would receive this tutoring outside of their regular Language Arts instruction. Volunteer tutors from the nearby university would provide explicit, systematic reading, spelling, and writing instruction in 1) letters/letter groups along with blending and spelling sounds, 2) identifying syllable types followed by practice segmenting, blending, and spelling syllables, 3) reading fluency, 4) vocabulary and semantics, 5) comprehension strategies, and 6) written expression.

The counselor also suggested offering a course elective similar to one that had shown promise at another middle school. The elective course curriculum and instruction aimed to promote African American well-being and youth leadership. Their tier 2 intervention was offered as a class three days a week to 8th grade African American students in their traditional public school setting. Students were exposed to and cherished African and African American culture and heritage regularly for one semester (Lewis, Sullivan, and Bybee, 2006). Sixty-five students were enrolled in the study. Thirty-two students were in the Emancipatory class, and 33 students were in the control group and received a regularly taught Life Skills course.

Emancipatory education means "freedom education." The curriculum focused on promoting leadership and social progress for their Black students and addressed practical ways they could improve their lives and their communities (Lewis, Sullivan, & Bybee, 2006, p 10). The instructor used lectures, discussions, group projects, videos, music, guest speakers, and traditional African ceremonies to facilitate learning.

The empowering curriculum of the intervention was designed to enrich students' skills. The study found that the intervention also improved the students' school connectedness and drive to succeed academically, along with increasing their students' involvement and efforts to create positive social changes in comparison to the control group. Research shows that there is a link between students who feel they belong in school and their drive to succeed in school (Lewis, Sullivan, & Bybee, 2006, p 20).

The counselor asked everyone, "Doesn't it make sense that the more a student feels connected, the more motivated he or she will be to achieve in school?"

He recommended that Austin Middle School offer an optional elective course similar to the one in the study. He suggested that it be open to all students, and that their low performing students would be formally invited and given first priority; they could be from any cultural background. Every student who signs up for the class would receive a description of the course with a permission slip to be signed by the student and guardian so that students will be able to participate in activities and field trips. Students enrolled in the class would brainstorm and vote on ways they would like to make noticeable changes in the school to promote community, school pride, and increase mutual respect. He ended, "The goals of the African American elective should be to help our students feel more connected to the African and African American cultures and their school with the hope that the students in this elective will develop their pride in our school and in themselves."

DECIDE INTERVENTIONS FOR YOUR TARGET STUDENTS (TIER 3)

Schools may want to offer more intensive intervention to students experiencing the greatest difficulties. Tier 3 provides more intensive intervention in small groups or one-to-one settings. It is intended to address difficulties of students with the highest needs. In this way, schools can develop a plan to address the needs of the most challenging students. What type of small group or one-to-one intervention will you use? Look to research and to what other schools have tried. What would be a good fit for your school?

Example

The other counselor continued by sharing the following tier 3 intervention. It was a *more intense level of intervention* that addressed the needs of one school's students who were coping with poverty, parents' substance abuse, parent criminality, and family violence. Students received intervention in smaller group settings to work on coping and developing resiliency. School counselors addressed issues like poor academics, expulsion, suspension, teenage pregnancies, and absenteeism during group counseling to prevent high school dropouts and improve the academic performance of African American students (Bemak, Chung, & Siroskey-Sabdo, 2005, p 377).

The counselor described how the intervention and study focused on seven 10th grade students who met once a week for 45 minutes. The school counselors in the study used an Empowerment Groups for Academic Success (EGAS) approach whereby students decided the topics for their group discussions. "By using the EGAS approach, group members developed ownership and had choices about discussing personal and social problems that were directly related to poor school behavior and performance and low attendance rates" (Bemak, Chung, & Siroskey-Sabdo, 2005, p 381). Accustomed to being told what to do, the students initially found this unusual. "This was the first step to empowerment, whereby the group members engaged in a partnership and actual ownership of the group process and content rather than responding to authority that rested solely with the facilitators. This is in line with a shift in which participants increasingly guide their own decisions and process" (ibid, p 382).

The counselor proposed that Austin Middle School offer a similar tier 3 intervention for any of their students who are struggling with family violence, substance abuse, and criminality. She articulated how group counseling in their school setting would help their at-risk students become more aware, cope better, and develop resiliency. In turn, this would have a positive effect on their grades, relationships with others, and promote more responsible behaviors.

MONITOR PROGRESS

Effective schools assess and monitor the progress of all students and teachers in the areas of academic achievement and discipline. Frequently monitoring the progress of each individual is critical to measuring the effectiveness of our actions, instruction, curriculum, and materials. The purpose of collecting data is so that we can take a pulse of our teaching practices, instruction, and their impact. This in turn can be used as a tool to base decisions and alter what we are doing.

Example

The assistant principal at Austin Middle School recommended that the entire staff receive professional development over the topics in Step 10 Address Patterns of Inappropriate Behavior. He also suggested that they continue tracking the referrals and in-school suspension rates of all their students. Teachers and students would supply the following notes with every referral and suspension for learning and prevention purposes. The teacher and student will both 1) define their behaviors, 2) note if either took what was said or done personally, 3) hypothesize what functions their behaviors served and list possible reasons and antecedents, 4) share the strategies they both used or should have used. Using this method, they could monitor their progress and measure the effectiveness of the teachers' actions, instruction, and practices, along with the students' behaviors and strategies.

Also, every student receiving reading intervention would be assessed weekly in reading fluency rates and comprehension rates. This would be done by the volunteer university students who will be implementing the reading, spelling, and writing interventions to their students.

SELECT A MENU OF CHOICES THAT SUPPORTS YOUR SCHOOL'S GOALS

When you design a school-wide intervention "cafeteria" style, you can create your own goals based on the needs of your students and what you would like to achieve. Once you've defined your goals, identified potential sources of support, developed plans for your tier 1, 2, and 3 interventions, and decided what data would be collected and monitored, you're ready to create a visual, like Figure 19.3. Faculty can refer to it and keep everyone focused. Under each goal is a menu of choices that will support your school's goals. See the following Figure 19.3 Goals with a Menu of Choices as an example.

Example

The staff at Austin Middle School created the following "Goals with a Menu of Choices."

Figure 19.3   Goals with a Menu of Choices

Improve School Culture	Increase Teacher Success	Increase Parent Involvement and Support	Increase Student Success
Cultivate cultural intelligence of administration and teachers through professional development Identify and address systematic practices that hinder targeted students' academic and behavioral successes. Ask teachers to identify and address curriculum that would be culturally insensitive to students' cultures. Infuse curriculum with contributions and perspectives of students' cultures.	Cultivate cultural intelligence in classroom environments. Improve teachers' perceptions of students. Provide teachers with materials and reading and behavioral interventions. Differentiate classroom instruction to increase teachers' rate of success teaching students of all abilities: - Increase students' feelings of success during instruction. - Provide immediate feedback in an encouraging manner.	Cultivate cultural intelligence by interacting with parents and families. Improve parents' and families' perceptions of teachers and staff by welcoming parents and families. Offer volunteer opportunities. Provide multiple opportunities to communicate and build rapport with families to cultivate trust and respect. Encourage family members to be facilitators of learning and advocates for their children.	Cultivate cultural intelligence of the students. Provide students with Tier 1, 2, and 3 interventions to: 1) narrow academic achievement gaps in students' test scores, 2) increase student progress, 3) decrease discipline rates, and 4) increase high school readiness. Use assessment data to monitor progress, and if rates of proficiency do not increase, then make adjustments and alter instruction. Improve students' perceptions of teachers, administration, school, and self.

Improve School Culture	Increase Teacher Success	Increase Parent Involvement and Support	Increase Student Success
Establish a school mission with goals, traditions, team building experiences, and opportunities for open discussions.	- Increase student engagement, interaction, and responses through questioning and checking for understanding.	Improve teachers' perceptions of their students' families and backgrounds.	Cultivate students' school connectedness and school pride.
Provide professional development that addresses instructional strategies and curriculum issues.	- Use faster presentation rates.	Understand parents' anger and refrain from judging.	Offer an African Studies elective that motivates, inspires, encourages, and fosters resilient behavior via motivational guest speakers, workshops, and activities (involving team-building, goal setting, decision-making, and leadership opportunities).
Publicly recognize staff members who are supportive, inspirational, relevant, spirited, collaborate well with others, and are leaders in initiatives.	- Include diagrams, illustrations, video clips, and photos throughout instruction. - Give examples and non-examples. - Color-code or highlight during lessons to distinguish similarities and differences.	Provide parents with materials and opportunities to learn from workshops, websites, and newsletters.	

CONSIDER THESE MENU CHOICES FOR YOUR SCHOOL

Your school may want to consider creating similar goals and menu of choices as the hypothetical Austin Middle School. Whether you choose to, or not, read through Figure 19.3 and imagine how you might adapt or modify goals and choices for your school.

Cultivate Cultural Intelligence

We often think culture is defined by race only. However, people within a culture can share similar backgrounds, experiences, social/emotional characteristics, language, religion, (family) values, or race. Many people may staunchly identify with two or more cultures.

People of the same culture often have similar belief systems, values, preferences, and needs. Schools and work places can address needs and promote the wellbeing of their students and employees by striving to increase cultural intelligence. Austin Middle School exemplifies how a school can increase their cultural IQ to promote the academic, social, and emotional well-being of African Americans. Imagine how cultural intelligence could also improve the outcomes of other cultures in your school, such as immigrants, LGBTQ, dyslexia, etc.

School curriculum has evolved over 400 years and lacks non-European contributions, perspectives, and influences. Schools can ensure that the African American history in their school curriculum covers more than slavery. Imagine the effects of learning about your people's slavery and oppression year after year. How empowering is that?

I am not African American; however, as a woman I remember how I felt when I learned women could not vote, own a house or land, and other inequalities. I felt shame and resentment for how women had been oppressed and violated. I was humiliated to learn that women's fates were controlled and in the hands of men. It was demeaning to hear repeatedly, alone or married, we were powerless.

Each year, I realized the inequalities, submissiveness, and oppression that still existed and how I struggled personally. In my mid-30's I journaled:

"Being a member of a group with a history of oppression is something I have had to overcome in my lifetime. In high school I would wince when being taught about women's suffrage, unequal pay for the same (or superior) work in the workforce, etc. What happens to us when we repeatedly hear the same messages over and over? And, how did I assume roles and scripts? Through introspection and self-help books, I dissected dominance, submission, authority, and differences, so that I can be the healthy wife, mother, teacher, citizen that I have actively shaped myself to be" (Hunter, 2006).

Likewise, when society teaches Black youths to downplay their own culture's experiences and the importance of the historic and modern problems surrounding their ethnic group, research suggests that their behavior and emotional well-being may be significantly affected (Lewis, 2006, p 4). Black students are taught almost every year they were (are) oppressed, could not vote, received no pay for their work. What happens to them when they repeatedly hear messages such as these over and over? Young Black students begin to wonder if they are assuming roles and scripts.

We must balance the negative with positive somehow. Even though every year I received historical facts about how women were oppressed, violated, controlled by men, and powerless, the potent doses of poison were delivered by teachers who were mostly women. They almost always followed with a sympathetic note, reminding us, girls, how it's no longer that way. They always said, "It's still not fair today, but conditions improve each generation. You will have more opportunities than I had." Hence, the sting I felt was soothed with words of hope and a give 'em hell message. In contrast, when we would talk about slavery, sharecropping, literacy tests required for voting, nothing was said, no words of hope, just awkward silences. Really, we must balance the negative poison with positive. We must deliver an antidote.

The antidote is cultivating cultural intelligence and plowing through the biases that contribute to social stratification and educational inequality. We can sow school cultures that produce empowered human beings who will become thriving citizens of our world. We have to dig deep and examine our academic, disciplinary, and social processes, systems, philosophies, and conventions. Are they embedded with biases that are stifling growth or creating blight in our children and teenagers?

Racism is more than just individual acts of unkindness or visible public events. Racism is also in the form of systems that have been set up and developed in ways that create racial dominance, and bias can be invisible to the eyes of unsuspecting onlookers. Yes, in our turn-of-the-21st century American life, African Americans are still struggling with racism. It was embedded in school systems from when they were originally created by Whites for Whites - with lasting visible and invisible effects.

Schools that provide professional development opportunities that foster the cultural intelligence of teachers are making an investment that pays its dividends in the academic success of our schools' students. Cultural professional development that stimulates change in faculty includes 1) exercises in self-awareness of one's values, beliefs, and behaviors, 2) understanding culturally diverse values, beliefs, and behaviors by making connections, and 3) skill development that fosters successful interactions with students and families from diverse cultures (Chan, 1990). This kind of professional development can help staff and teachers explore our academic, disciplinary, and social processes, systems, philosophies, and conventions. By increasing our cultural IQ, we will also have the power to administer the antidote for social injustice to achieve educational equalities of our students.

Improve Teacher Perceptions of Students

I was picking up my daughter from elementary school one day. As I stood waiting for her, I saw a teacher who became angry when her student (who was African American and in the 2nd grade) told her he had missed his bus. She yelled at him and loudly asked him how he could possibly have missed the bus. He stood quietly with his body facing her, but looking to the side of her. His silence and lack of eye contact made her more outraged. She said to him, "Young man, you better listen to me. Do not look away. You look at me when I talk to you." His body started to sway back and forth, but he did not look at her or say a word. She said, "That's it. You're going to see the principal."

The teacher thought her student was rude by not looking at her, so she threatened to take him to the principal. Why was it so important for him to look at her? Because, it is customary for White Americans to maintain eye contact with the person speaking to them. I wanted to tell her, in some cultures it is considered disrespectful to look someone in the eyes when they are in trouble. It may be a sign of respect for her, but in other cultures, making eye contact with the aggressor challenges their dominance and communicates contempt. I honestly believe, he thought his lack of eye contact was his way of being respectful, and he shutdown because of her hostility.

Also, too often teachers equate "looking" with "hearing." I wanted to tell the teacher, we do not hear with our eyes. Just because a student doesn't look at you, doesn't mean he or she is not listening or being disrespectful. I should have spoken up for the student or at least reported the teacher's behavior. But I didn't. I regret that deeply. I hope this may prevent others from making the same mistake.

Most White children enter schools with the language and interpersonal skills, vocabulary, and behaviors of the dominant culture, thus they enter school with an advantage. In contrast, students from nondominant cultures enter school with language and interpersonal skills, vocabulary, and behaviors of another culture. Rather than being perceived as valuable, teachers too often perceive these differences as behaviors of "failure" and "rudeness." Consequently, General Education and Special Ed teachers may *unknowingly* give different treatment to some students because of cultural similarities and differences.

An action, gesture, or speech can convey meaning in one culture, but something different in another. When teachers are aware, we have a set of communication styles, pragmatics, and body language that influences how we motivate others and give and receive respect, then we are more likely to increase our cultural intelligence. If we possess a high cultural IQ in classrooms and work environments, then we can interact with someone outside of our culture and interpret the meaning of an action, gesture, or speech as if we were from the same culture, even though we are not. The higher our cultural IQ, the less likely we will misunderstand others in classrooms and work environments. Plus, we'll be less likely to show our lack of understanding in our demeanors, and less likely to offend our students and coworkers. As a result, we'll be more likely to cultivate respect and cooperation.

Let's say for example, a student in your classroom suddenly talks excitedly about something. If speaking calmly is valued in your culture, then that student's behavior may be considered rude or annoying. Being aware that different (family) cultures have different communication styles can help you in situations like this. Rather than seeing it as rude, view it as expressive and spontaneous. Most importantly, check your body language and prevent yourself from doing things, such as narrowing your eyes in a judging manner to the student. Refocus how you look at certain behaviors and keep your attention on the task at hand.

Similarly, our culture's values and beliefs may also be different from a student or coworker. Yet, if we have a high cultural intelligence, then the person outside our culture can say, believe, and value something that we may personally disagree with, but we can refrain from judging them, their values, and beliefs. In turn, it is less likely we will offend our students and coworkers and more likely they will respect us and become more motivated.

Differentiate Instruction

We, teachers, can improve our students' success, even when they have had a history of not meeting our expectations academically and/or behaviorally. Step 18 Honor Their Differences explains in detail how we can differentiate classroom instruction in specific ways to ultimately make teaching easier and more effective. Some of the benefits include: improved learning, respect, cooperation, and a significant decrease in undesirable behaviors in the classroom.

"The teacher who laments, 'I'd like to reinforce that student but he/she just doesn't ever do the right thing' is ignoring the teacher's role in instruction. It is the teacher's job to design instruction so the students are likely to be successful. Failures indicate a need for altering instruction; simply insisting that students with histories of failure be responsible for turning things around by 'trying harder' is illogical and will not succeed" (Scott, Nelson, & Liaupsin, 2001, 318). Examples of differentiating instruction validated by research are: maintaining a high level of student engagement (Levy & Chard, 2010), faster presentation rates (Sutherland & Wehby, 2001), and designing instruction so that academically failing students can actively respond during class time instruction to increase their attentiveness and help them feel successful on a daily basis (Sutherland & Wehby, 2001). When we alter our instruction in these ways, we will more effectively meet the needs of our students. Consequently, our students will become more successful.

When a student is failing in the classroom, feelings of success are fundamental reinforcers, and they are vital for sustained learning (Scott, Nelson, & Liaupsin, 2001).

> Not all individuals, as children or adults, have consistent experiences that link their actions with outcomes. A child who studies hard but does not do well on the spelling test, an adult who completes a vocational training program but cannot get a job in that field, or a family that complains to their landlord about broken plumbing but gets no response learn over time that their actions do not make a difference—that they do not have control or influence over their lives.

> From pp 57-58 of Developing Cross-Cultural Competence: A Guide for Working with Children and Their Families, Fourth Edition, Lynch and Hanson ©2011 Brookes Publishich Co. Used with permissio

This quote stresses the importance of frequently and consistently supplying reinforcement to underperforming students' efforts. Likewise, we can be more effective teachers by designing instruction whereby our "disruptive" students can receive reinforcement *during learning* on a *daily* basis and, hence, link their success to their academic effort.

"Good" behavior can be fostered through providing consistent positive feedback that is specific and links the positive results to the student's actions. Differentiating instruction in this manner is one way we can transform our students' undesirable behaviors into more scholarly behaviors.

Here are other examples of differentiating instruction (see Step 18 Honor Their Differences for more details and examples):

- Increase students' feelings of success during instruction
- Provide immediate feedback in an encouraging manner
- Increase student engagement, interaction, and responses through questioning and checking for understanding
- Use faster presentation rates during lessons
- Include diagrams, illustrations, video clips, and photos throughout instruction
- Give examples and non-examples
- Color-code and highlight to distinguish similarities and differences

Focus on the Needs of the Child and Family

James Kauffman has published several articles regarding emotional and behavioral disorders, learning disabilities, and special education. He explains how family factors such as parental drug and alcohol abuse, parental incarceration, family violence, abuse, lack of parental care, and trauma can affect children's behaviors and contribute to low academic achievement. However, he cautions that these factors do not set a child's future in stone. I agree with Kauffman's assertions that family characteristics and experiences do not dictate students' futures. Nor does it serve students when teachers say that their lack of success is due to parents, family characteristics, and home lives. When teachers, administrators, and staff blame parents, the focus is no longer about teaching and helping the children learn adaptive skills and appropriate behaviors. When parents are blamed and shamed, their focus shifts from cooperating with the teachers and staff to defending their son or daughter, their parenting skills, or family circumstances (Kauffman, 2005). When everyone's focus, energy, and time move away from the student, then the child is the one who is hurt. Isn't the purpose of our meetings and communications with each other to collaborate and figure out ways we can help, not harm, our children and teenagers? By keeping our focus on the needs of the child, we can prevent this irony from occurring.

Involve Parents

Research shows that parental involvement and partnering with parents contribute to our children's academic and behavioral successes. Teachers can build effective partnerships by welcoming parents, communicating a fresh start, inviting them to volunteer in the classroom, building rapport with parents, trusting and respecting them, and viewing them as facilitators of learning (Ortiz, 2006).

Cultivate School Connectedness and School Pride

Successful schools unify their culturally and linguistically diverse students and staff by creating and cultivating their own unique school culture. Teachers, staff, and students can establish a school mission with goals, traditions, team building experiences, and opportunities for open discussions to create their own unified school culture.

School campaigns and mottos, such as "Together…but not the same" can communicate positive messages of unity to the students. Teachers can take existing lesson plans and point out positives of different cultures. They can identify and address curriculum that would be culturally insensitive to students' cultures and infuse the curriculum with contributions and perspectives of their students' cultures. These are all restorative actions that incubate feelings of connectedness and school pride in students.

Foster Resilient Behavior

A student's frustration can manifest itself in "bad" behavior. I challenge teachers to think of "bad" behavior as a distress signal, to explore the root causes of the misbehavior, and, more importantly, to examine what could be triggering the undesired behavior. Take for example, a student who acted out because his pencil lead broke. Did the child act out because his pencil lead broke? Or was it something else? What really triggered that response? Was it anxiety from his or her inability to meet the teacher's, the parent's, or the student's own expectations? Or fear of failure? Or family events we may not be aware of? Resiliency is vital to persevering through adversity, forging forward in spite of experiencing difficulties. Interventions for at-risk students should focus on fostering resilient behaviors.

One way we can foster resilient behavior is by creating a paradigm shift in our struggling students. Communicate the blessings that occur from hard work, hard times, and adversity.

> Achieving, when the odds are stacked against you, can be a tremendous gift. What all you have to do, how you have to be, just to keep up with everyone, is so hard. But the rewards do come. How so? Because whether you realize it or not, all that time you were working so hard to catch up, you were conditioning yourself to work harder, strive harder than everyone else…which later pushes you to go further than everyone else. So don't let it get you down. It can be a beautiful thing. (Hunter, 2006)

School staff can invite professionals and business leaders as guest speakers to encourage, motivate, and inspire students to set goals, analyze their choices, and become leaders in the school, community, and workplace. Some of the topics could include linking good decisions to success, turning failures into success, sharing stories of perseverance, hard work, and determination, etc.

Increase Student Success

Evidence from a number of studies show that teachers are more likely to have negative communications and serve more punitive consequences to students who are less academically proficient (Scott, Nelson, & Liaupsin, 2001, p 313). As a result, underperforming students respond by escaping, many times through undesirable behaviors. Students and teachers create cycles of escalating behaviors and disciplinary removal from the classroom. The irony and reality of this cycle is that students who are struggling academically need *more* rigorous instruction as opposed to being removed from the environment of learning (Ibid, p 314).

Teachers can break chronic patterns of behavior with students who are failing academically by combining scientifically research-based practices like providing proper interventions and increasing opportunities for students to feel success. Instructors can see the power of giving extra help and praise to a "good" student. We can see how it can make a student beam and give them motivation to try harder. So, why do some teachers withhold strategies combined with creating feelings of success from "bad" students? Sometimes we know what to do, but we choose to withhold it from a student or certain students. If this describes you, take a moment to reread Step 13 Bridge the Distance to understand why and Step 14 Build Character to help your student(s) become more of the person you'd like for them to be. If you believe they're unreachable, reread Step 15 Be Relevant to motivate them. If you don't know how to help them, reread Step 16 Identify the Obstacles Preventing Success to understand the root cause of their difficulties and Step 17 Remove the Obstacles Preventing Success and Step 18 Honor Their Differences to understand how to overcome their educational and behavioral challenges. Administrators may want to design professional development around these topics.

DESIGN AND DEVELOP EACH TIER ONE AT A TIME

It is up to individual schools and school districts to meet the needs of students. Implementing all three tiers of the three-tiered model may seem time-consuming in our world of quick fixes, fast food, and drive-thru's. However, your school can start one tier at a time. You can design and develop each tier "cafeteria" style. You can create a menu of research-based practices that fits your unique school's goals and increase your students' success and achievement.

A school system is a group that consists of students, teachers, administrators, counselors, librarians, coaches, etc. They are all individuals, and yet together, they, interact with each other to perform an overall, vital function. These separate forces form a network and serve a common purpose.

Just like our circulatory and nervous systems, school systems are also made up of living parts. And because school systems are living, they are capable of growing, evolving, and healing. Like any living organism, schools must also be fed a healthy diet and given fresh air to thrive and produce healthy offspring. By focusing and developing one area or tier at a time, we can grow, evolve, and heal the current systems we have in place in our schools. As a result, the individual parts will unify to make our school body healthier and more successful.

Lesson 19 | Identify Goals and Sources of Support

 Faculty, PTAs, Campus Committees, and administrators. can complete the following activity to increase success in achieving school-wide goals.

Identify the specific area(s) you want to address in your school:

- Increase student success
- Improve school culture
- Increase teacher success
- Increase parent involvement and support

What specific goal(s) would you like to achieve?

Identify who could be potential sources of support?

How could you share your vision with potential sources of support? How could you communicate urgency and excitement?

What goals will you assess and track? How will you monitor your progress?

What are the possible sources of opposition? How will you respond? What will you say and do? How will you remain positive?

Journal 19 | Create a Menu of Choices

 Faculty, PTAs, Campus Committees, and administrators journal:

Meet with possible sources of support and go over your notes from Lesson 19 Identify Goals and Sources of Support. Together, customize your Menu of Choices.

Journal how the Menu of Choices could meet the goal(s). Draft a calendar of events. Make a list of to do's.

STEP 20 | ADVOCATE, BECAUSE IT'S THE RIGHT THING TO DO

SCREEN AND IDENTIFY CHILDREN

Years of research and professional development of teachers are helping schools provide students with better reading instruction. However, schools are still failing to identify students with dyslexia, dysgraphia, dyscalculia, ADHD, English learners, etc.

Without identification, many children are not receiving the proper instruction in written expression, spelling, math, reading fluency, and classroom behaviors. Therefore, it is reasonable for a parent or teacher to request that an underperforming student be screened. Diagnostic assessments will show weaknesses and student characteristics that can lead to identification.

Once a student's challenges are identified, teachers and parents can begin to provide instruction and support that more directly address the student's needs. Examples of support can include intervention to address weak areas, differentiated instruction in the classroom setting, and 504 Accommodations in the classroom and during testing.

Many parents and teachers are fearful of "labeling" their child. If this describes you, please note that just because a child has a label such as dyslexia or ADHD, it does not sentence that person to a life of not being able to read or sit still. With early intervention, 504 Accommodations, and differentiated instruction, all students can become proficient and successful in the classroom. Also note, a "label" does not have to be permanent. You may identify your child so you can advocate for support and then remove the identification and supports later.

I wrote the following in my journal years ago describing the blessings that can come from giving a difficulty a name.

Journal 7-14-05

It was like walking across a bridge to a place I'd never been before. And, it was no longer possible to go back to the way it was. The bridge I'd crossed had disappeared. I understood clearly that I was in new territory, and I wanted to understand this new place. In the process, I began to understand my children's strengths and weaknesses so that I could healthily address their weaknesses and foster their strengths. As a result, our lives began to change.

Before I crossed the bridge, I was frustrated and hostile when I would work with my sons. After crossing, I practiced patience. And for my sons, before they knew they had dyslexia, they would call themselves stupid when they experienced difficulties related to their dyslexia. But after I explained to them that they had dyslexia, it was as if a burden had been lifted. Over time they began to understand their difficulties were not related to a lack of intelligence. They began to see just how smart they really are. They began to understand why they had to work harder than everyone else and, subsequently, they went through an academic growth spurt.

Laurie Hunter

If your child cannot be screened or identified, for whatever reason, you can always assess their learning style. There are many online tools that can help you determine your child's learning style profile. You can use this valuable information to advocate for instruction that can make a difference for your child.

If your child has been screened and does not qualify, when you know he or she should have, request another screening the following year at the very beginning, when school starts. Be relentless all year long and fight for what you know is right by using logic and tact.

If that school flat out refuses to provide intervention to your child, become best friends with your child's teacher, volunteer in the classroom, and learn how to provide intervention to your child yourself. Learn how you can become a facilitator of learning. Your child's teacher will notice and match your efforts. Teachers will make sure your child learns when they see you busting your butt. The time you put towards this goal will save you time later. Your time spent now is an investment that will pay off later. We will be given a second chance at a career, but we will not be given a second chance to raise our children.

LEARN HOW POWERFUL YOU CAN BE

The real problem is not dyslexia, dysgraphia, or ADHD or learning a new language or "bad" parents and teachers. Rather, it's the feeling of powerlessness that parents and teachers feel. When our children and students struggle, we feel powerless.

If teachers, and especially parents, only knew that we have the most powerful effect on the academic success of our children. Indeed, it is the people closest who can help the most, hands down. Yet we, teachers and parents of struggling students, feel powerless and everyone continues to struggle!

And if that's not enough, society gives us built-in excuses that reinforce why we should give up… "Public schools are to blame," "We both work and there's just no time," "I don't have the money for a tutor," and "The school just doesn't have the time or resources." We are using these damaging myths as excuses for not fixing the problem.

The real problem: Powerlessness.

The real solution: Understand and learn how powerful we can be.

ADVOCATE WITH LOGIC AND POSITIVE ENERGY

If your school is not able to provide the support your child or student needs, your involvement is critical. I created this book to empower parents, tutors, and teachers. You can take what you've learned in Steps 16, 17, and 18 to advocate for your child(ren). You can have an impact on your child's achievement in reading, spelling, writing, math, behaviors, wherever you place your energy.

Years ago, when I realized my sons had dyslexia, most teachers and principals didn't have a clue what dyslexia was. Nor did they know what to do with a student who had dyslexia. I couldn't let my children suffer, so I learned everything I could about it (Step 16 Identify the Obstacles Preventing Success), even how to provide intervention for it (Step 17 Remove the Obstacles Preventing Success). I thought that by blasting the school principal, counselor, and teachers with fact after fact they would understand logic. At first it made them dig in their heels more, and they resisted screening my sons for dyslexia. I kept working with my sons and advocating for them to be identified. I did not give up, and I continued to inform them in positive ways.

I realized during my struggles, advocating for my children, my problem was not with the teachers. Indeed, it was not the teachers I was fighting; it was the school culture and their procedures. For four years I labored with school procedures to get dyslexia screening, identification, intervention, and 504 Modifications for my sons. Do you realize that is the same amount of time it takes to get an undergrad degree? And that is the amount of time it took me to get through this process.

It dawned on me that the principal, counselor, and some teachers were not woven of the same fibers; that's why they didn't automatically understand me, and I wondered if they ever would. However, I realized sharing the information and offering to be a part of the solution helped them to grow new fibers. I waited for them to grow and continued to do what I knew was the right thing to do. Eventually, my sons were screened and identified with dyslexia. Other parents and teachers saw and heard and began to advocate for their own children. You can too.

During my years of advocating for my children, there were times when I felt powerless. I was tempted to respond in a most disrespectful manner. You may feel powerless, frustrated, and angry also, but resist the urge to be disrespectful. Make a conscious effort to not be reckless or gossip about how bad a teacher or school is or threaten their jobs. Instead, be thought provoking, caring, and realize your power without using angry words, tears, or intimidation. An emotional plea with tears will get you nowhere. Angry words or intimidation will get you caught in a conflict cycle that wastes precious time. Parents and teachers, use data and research to voice what is right for our children and communicate with logic and tact. Knowledge is power.

Most schools and teachers know when their instruction needs to change to meet the needs of our students. However, many continue to provide the same curriculum and methods. Teachers who do not want to improve their art are like artists who do not want to create anything more beautiful than they've already created. I understand many teachers have their value systems and preferred methods in place, and they may be resistant to change. However, teachers who refuse to improve their methods and techniques are like engineers who use design flaws that could collapse buildings and harm people. We can't always continue to do something because it's easier or because it's how it's always been done.

Unfortunately, inflexible, ineffective school cultures and procedures are hard to change. School cultures are not tangible things we can physically reconstruct; they are mentalities. And if we want to change them, it will require a series of compelling logic and courageous actions. People like you and me will have to stand up and say that we will no longer operate in a fashion that is not in the best interests of our children.

> I have discovered that life is not a series of great heroic acts. Life at its best is a matter of consistent goodness and decency, doing without fanfare that which needed to be done when it needed to be done. I have observed that it is not the geniuses that make the difference in this world. I have observed that the work of the world is done largely by men and women of ordinary talent who have worked in an extraordinary manner.

> Excerpt from One Bright Shining Hope, page 24 ©2006 by Gordon B. Hinckley
> Deseret Book Company. Used by Permission

Lesson 20 | Advocate for the "Active Ingredient"

Parents and teachers should advocate for children to receive instruction that will effectively increase proficiency in the areas they struggle. If you're not sure what those areas might be, then it will be quite difficult to advocate for your child. If that's the case, review the three guiding questions in Step 17 Remove the Obstacles Preventing Success. These questions will help you identify the "active ingredients" that will address the root cause and increase proficiency.

Faculty and parents can complete the following activity to advocate for their children.

Schedule a meeting and advocate for the "active ingredient." If a school is reluctant or cannot provide intervention, a parent or tutor can challenge their institution to supply their child with effective intervention at school.

Anticipate excuses you may hear. (The school has only so many resources, we are already spread so thin, we are not required by law to serve your student, etc.)

- What are possible ways you can respond?
- What are some possible solutions?
- How can you be a part of the solution?
- How will you not be a part of the problem?
- How can you phrase most of what you want to say in the form of questions?
- What are other ways you can prepare yourself for their resistance?

Journal 20 | Provide the "Active Ingredient"

Faculty, instructor or parent journals:

If you fail in your efforts to advocate for your child or student, journal how your words and actions may still have an effect on the future. How can you continue to plant seeds of ideas in their brains?

While you are waiting for the school to provide proper instruction or if the instruction the school provides falls short of what is needed, then a parent, teacher, or tutor should feel empowered to provide intervention themselves. Journal what you can do to help your student(s) during, before, or after school and over the summer and weekends.

STEP 21 | **ACHIEVE SUCCESS**

INCREASE YOUR AWARENESS

Have you ever found yourself so immersed in a book or movie that you fell so deeply into it that you forgot about your worries and stress? I want you to "get lost" in your own life in the same way. I don't want to transport you to another world. I want to transport you back into yours...and to help you become a full participant in the greatest adventure, your life.

You may have stresses, financial instability, illness, or broken relationships. Doesn't a good book or movie have those as well? We root for the good guys to rise above their challenges. Everyone has a story; everyone has to overcome challenges. As you are reading this, I am rooting for you. It is my wish that my book has not only helped you attain more respect and cooperation, but that it may also help you mend a relationship or overcome one of your life's biggest conflicts. Follow the tenets of this book, and it will be a defibrillator that can revive you and your relationships.

Moreover, I want you to fall in love with life again, appreciate your child, students, job, and your roles in life. And when it's time for you to leave this world, I want you to leave behind treasures that are not possessions.

What is space? Is it the distance between one object and another? Or, is it the nothingness that exists between the two objects? Memories can be viewed in much the same way. Nothing exists between two memories. Think back and reflect on your own childhood. You may recall one memory after another, and you can even put them in chronological order. But, what is between each memory? Nothing. We can fill time with few memories and a lot of nothingness in between. Or, we can make more memories with less nothingness in between. Moving forward, ask yourself, "How can I live a fuller and more complete life? How can I work towards making more memories now, so in the future I will reflect on a fuller, more complete life?"

By recognizing the following realizations, you can make sweeping changes to living a fuller, more complete and successful life.

- Our thoughts, words, and actions can foster or prevent our success.
- Our egos can prevent us from connecting with others or not.
- We can address our weaknesses and foster our strengths or not.

- We can create our own definition of success or accept someone else's.
- We have been handed "scripts" that we can follow or not.

TOSS THE SCRIPTS FOR HEALTHIER RELATIONSHIPS

Disrespect and lack of cooperation can stem from our children and teens' feelings of powerlessness, anger, or anxiety. In other words, when they experience failure and/or lack of power, it can result in anger or anxiety, which can come out in undesirable actions like backtalk and physical aggression. They may say hurtful words or become sarcastic.

Children have been handed "scripts" that they think they need to follow. They borrow wording from TV, movies, friends, family members, and you. They look to these sources to help them communicate how they feel. Over the years, TV, movies, and people make them think they have to behave in certain ways in certain situations. Sometimes, it is irresistible to imitate what someone else said.

You know, you have been handed scripts too. Analyze what you think, say, and do. Sometimes, isn't it tempting to say something sarcastic? Do some words just automatically come out? If so, I want you to change your thinking, and I challenge you to speak genuinely. Scripts lie. True feelings that are said with humility do not. The more you stick to scripts, the less life you will live. When we dump the scripts and abandon verbal and body reflexes, we will speak from the heart, have more genuine conversations, and experience more fulfilling relationships with our children, spouses, family, and friends.

What if during a heated argument, you threw down the script and said something genuine. Your child or teen may still yell back or say something after you've put yourself out there – and that's what we're afraid of, and that's often what keeps us from being genuine. But, if we throw down the scripts and speak with open hearts, over time, others will begin to throw down their scripts and be more genuine back.

It is widely believed that as children grow older, peers will become a bigger influence than a parent. However, more studies show that the parent remains the most influential factor in a child's life through high school. Teachers with certain qualities are a close second. It is the parents and teachers who are firm, strict, get mad, hold their children and teens accountable, and deliver consequences along with messages of love or care that have a profound effect. To have that kind of effect, it will require us to communicate carefully with our words, body language, and tone.

It is our job as parents and educators to be firm, have high expectations, and hold our children and students accountable. When our children and students accuse us of being "mean," we can respond by telling them we are not "punishing" them because we're getting pleasure out of it, but because we care. We must also communicate that if would be easier for us to do nothing; but because we love them, we have to be strict and hold them accountable. Being firm and allowing our children to suffer consequences are important for the development of their academic, personal, and emotional well-being.

When we first start conveying this to them, it may appear they are not listening to us. They may get mad and respond in unfavorable ways that may make us want to counter with sarcasm and anger. However, if we pair sarcasm and anger with being strict, then we run the risk of conjuring spite and rebelliousness. In contrast, if our firmness is paired with a message that says, "Look, I'm being this way because I care," then we will cultivate their trust in us, which in turn will healthily develop a good conscience, independence, self-discipline, and accountability.

> I'm being "mean" *because* I love you. If I didn't care about you, then I'd let you do whatever. Wouldn't that be easier? Wouldn't it be so much easier for me do nothing?
>
> But how would that help you grow? How would that help you prepare for the future?
>
> When you're older, I don't want you to say, "Why didn't you do a better job raising me?" I'm "mean" because I want you to say later in life, "Thanks for being good parent."
>
> A Loving Parent

Set limits, maintain your composure, and try to figure out what's behind the words. Ask questions that encourage them to share their feelings, and then get ready to listen. And then listen some more. We should be strict, firm, and hold our children to high expectations, along with authentically communicating that we care. It's a powerful combo.

CULTIVATE SUCCESS WITH YOUR THOUGHTS, WORDS, AND ACTIONS

Thoughts, words, and actions can either cultivate or prevent success. Study the following chart outlining the difference between successful and unsuccessful people's thoughts, words, and actions. Think about the different behaviors of people you know. When have you observed others thinking, saying, and doing these things? When have you thought, said, or done these? What behaviors stand in your way? How and when can you cue yourself to choose positive behaviors? How and when can you cue your child or student to choose them as well? Our thoughts, words, and actions can either cultivate success or they can prevent us from being successful in our endeavors.

Figure 21.1   Characteristics of Successful and Unsuccessful People
('The Success Indicator' Info-graphic 2012 by Mary Ellen Tribby, Founder of WorkingMomsOnly.com)
Adapted by Laurie Hunter)

Successful	Unsuccessful
Thoughts	**Thoughts**
I am grateful	I am prideful
I am forgiving	I hold grudges
I accept help when it is needed	I hold myself above others
Humble	Knows it all
Looks at things positively	Looks at things negatively
Words	**Words**
"Thank you"	"Look at me!"
"It's alright, I forgive you"	"It's your fault, go away"
"I could use your help"	"I can handle this myself"
Says compliments	Criticizes, gossips
Disagrees respectfully	Angrily disagrees
Actions	**Actions**
Holds one's self accountable	Blames others
Doesn't prejudge	Quick to judge others
Sets goals & makes to do lists	Doesn't set goals
Helps others succeed	Unconscious of others
Embraces change	Fears and resists change
Takes the initiative	Relies on others' approval
Keeps a journal	Doesn't journal
Asks questions	Doesn't ask questions

SET ASIDE YOUR EGO

Dear fellow teachers, tutors, and coaches, teaching is not about me or you. Whether you realize it or not, our students come to us with their worries, fears, and hopes concealed in their young brains and bodies. If we look carefully, we can see how they communicate their anxieties and dreams with their actions, words, or behaviors. For every child, it is different. Some will tell you openly, but most will mask their difficulties, appearing indifferent, apathetic, or even rebellious. For me, teaching is about actively setting aside my ego and connecting with those students. Each day, we should aim to be there for each student because every child has a story, even if they are not telling it to us. When I am teaching, I try to think in terms of what I can do instructionally and emotionally for each student. That gives me the faith that what I have chosen to do will impact each child. Thoughtful, caring instruction can make a difference in ways that we may not even be aware of. We may even think it is not making much of a difference and not worth all the time or energy.

Dear teachers, if we set aside our egos and aim each day for our challenging students to leave better than when they came to us, then it will add up to something significant. And more importantly, we will be part of creating a ripple effect that may not have happened if it weren't for us.

Cherokee Proverb

An old Cherokee told his grandson,
"My son, there is a battle between two wolves inside us all.
One is Evil. It is anger, envy, jealousy, sorrow, regret, greed, arrogance, self-pity, guilt, resentment, inferiority, lies, false pride, superiority, and ego. The other is Good. It is joy, peace, love, hope, serenity, humility, kindness, benevolence, empathy, generosity, truth, compassion and faith."

The boy thought about it, and asked, "Grandfather, which wolf wins?"

The old man quietly replied, "The one you feed."

Author Unknown

ADDRESS WEAKNESSES, FOSTER STRENGTHS, AND CULTIVATE SUCCESS

I, myself, have dyslexia. I struggled through the first half of my schooling. We, struggling students, mistakenly feel that we are stuck on the bottom rungs of the ladder of success. In spite of how hard we try, those feelings are reinforced with repeated failures. If that's not enough, we are also confronted by a mentality telling us that's where we're meant to be. Dear reader, it has taken me years to learn that *we all have the potential to move up (or down) that ladder of success.* As teachers and parents, we can actively help our struggling students to stop viewing themselves as being at the bottom of a *stationary* rung of a ladder. And as teachers and parents, we can strive to cultivate a healthier mentality *by providing instruction that builds skills* whereby a student at the bottom of the class can *escalate* and have the opportunity to *rise above* their current challenges.

Congratulations on making it through all the steps. Dear reader, I hope you revisit this book and the journals you have written. Why? In order to be effective, we must bring up the tenets of each step again and again as opportunities present themselves in our daily lives. Rereading this book and our journals will make that happen.

Every student needs an inspiration, someone who cares, and someone who will have patience, no matter what. Reread this book when you feel you need to practice patience or to inspire your child up a rung of the ladder. *No matter what has been preventing your child or student from being able to reach the next step up*, always search to understand, communicate positively, healthily address their weaknesses, and foster their strengths. The hard work you have done will last a lifetime. I promise you, lives will change, including your own. I can almost feel you smiling and saying to yourself, "It has. And it's going to keep getting better!"

I'd like to end with the words of Kirsten Sturgill Murphy:

> Life is a marathon. Some spots on the path are easier to run than others. Sometimes our pace is fast and sometimes it is slow. We sweat, we bleed, we limp, we run, we walk, we cry, we press on. And in our life's marathon, there are people lining the course cheering for us, supporting us, and encouraging us to push on and to press forward. Marathons aren't easy. Life is not easy. But in each, there are great blessings along the way as well as at the finish line. So, no matter what mile marker you may be at in your life marathon, remember: "You've got this!" "You Rock!" "Keep going!" "You're doing a great job!" "And you're not alone."

Everyone has a story, and I've just shared part of mine with you. Whether you're reading this for you, your child, a student, spouse, coworker, team member, or friend, know that I am rooting for you.

Lesson 21 | Your Homework

Instructor or parent can use Figure 21.2 Goal Sheet to write goals you would like to accomplish with your child or student.

Principal or administrator can write goals you'd like to accomplish in your schools.

Write down your goals on the following Figure 21.2 Goal Sheet. Write down the steps you can take towards making each goal happen. Then, take action.

Figure 21.2 Goal Sheet

Goals	Specific Actions I Will Take

Journal 21 | How Have You Succeeded? How Will You Succeed?

 Instructor or parent journals:

"Success" by Emerson redefines success in a meaningful way. Write how you have succeeded so far in life. What do you feel are your most important accomplishments? Write what you would like to achieve in the future.

Success

To laugh often and much; to win the respect of intelligent people and the affection of children; to earn the appreciation of honest critics and endure the betrayal of false friends; to appreciate beauty, to find the best in others; to leave the world a bit better, whether by a healthy child, a garden patch or a redeemed social condition; to know even one life has breathed easier because you have lived. This is to have succeeded.

Ralph Waldo Emerson

REFERENCES

Bemak, F., Chung, R., & Siroskey-Sabdo, L. (2005). Empowerment groups for academic success: An innovative approach to prevent high school failure for at-risk, urban African. *Professional School Counseling, 8*(5), 377-389.

Chan, S. (1990). Early intervention with culturally diverse families of infants and toddlers with disabilities. *Infants and Young Children,* 3(2), 78-87

Cooper, S. (2014). *Active Ingredient.* Email retrieved on December 4, 2014.

Covey, S. R. (2004). *The 8th habit: From effectiveness to greatness.* New York, NY: Free Press.

DeMario, M. (2018). Personal communication. Austin, TX

Dreikurs, R. & Stolz, V. (1991, 1964). *Children: The challenge: The classic work on improving parent-child relations-intelligent, humane, and eminently practical.* New York, NY: Penguin Publishing Group.

Eunice Kennedy Shriver National Institute of Child Health and Human Development, NIH, DHHS. (2001). *Put reading first: The research building blocks for teaching children to read.* Washington, DC: U.S. Government Printing Office.

Fiese, Bryan. (2005). *Rubbing People the Wrong Way.* Texas PTA Summer Leadership Seminar. Austin, TX.

Fifield, W. (2012, August). Ken Robinson's crusade, Teach your children well. *Costco Connection* 27(8), 32-35.

Foorman, B., Francis, D., Shaywitz, S., Shaywitz, B., & Fletcher, J. (1997). The case for early reading intervention. In B. Blachman (Ed.), *Foundations of Reading Acquisition and Dyslexia* (pp. 243-264). Mahwah, NJ: Lawrence Erlbaum.

Gorman, C. (2003, July 28). The new science of dyslexia. *Time,* 52-59.

Hallahan, D., Lloyd, J., Kauffman, J., Weiss, M., & Martinez, E. (2005). *Learning disabilities: Foundations, characteristics, and effective teaching.* 3rd edition. Boston, MA: Pearson.

Hinckley, G. (2006). *One bright shining hope.* Deseret Book Company: Salt Lake City, UT.

Hughes, G., Cowley, K., Copley, L., Finch, N., & Meehan, M. (2005). Evaluation of a multi-school pilot project designed to close achievement gaps. Appalachia Educational Laboratory Charleston, WV: AEL.

Hunter, L. (2005, 2006). Journal of Laurie Hunter.

Hunter, L. (2013). *Teach your child to read: A step-by-step guide for teachers and parents, 1st grade – 12th grade*. Austin, TX: Self-published instruction manual.

Hunter, L. (2008). *Evaluating the impact of an intervention on struggling readers*. The University of Texas at Austin, TX: Master's Thesis.

Kauffman, J. (2005). *Characteristics of emotional and behavioral disorders of children and youth*, 8th edition. Boston, MA: Pearson.

Kohn, A. (1999). *The schools our children deserve: moving beyond traditional classrooms and "tougher standards"*. New York, NY: Houghton Mifflin Company.

Levy, S. & Chard, D. (2010). Research on reading instruction for students with emotional and behavioural disorders. *International Journal of Disability, Development and Education, 48*(4), 429-444. http://dx.doi.org/10.1080/10349120120094301. Reprinted by permission of the publisher Taylor & Francis Ltd, http:www.tandfonline.com.

Lewis, K., Sullivan, C., & Bybee, D. (2006). An experimental evaluation of a school-based emancipatory intervention to promote African American well-being and youth leadership. *Journal of Black Psychology, 32*(1). 3-28.

Lynch, E. (2011). Developing cross-cultural competence. In E.W. Lynch & M.J. Hanson (Eds.), *Developing cross-cultural competency: A guide for working with children and their families* (4th ed.) (pp. 41-75). Baltimore, MD: Brookes Publishing.

Mehrabian, A. (1972). *Nonverbal communication*. Piscataway, NJ: Transaction Publishers.

Mestas & Peterson (1999). The Department of Education's Committee for Enhancing Cultural Competence in Colorado. Personal communication.

Murphy, Kirsten. "My Reflective Post" dated 1 November 2015.

Nolte, D. & Harris, R. (1998). *Children learn what they live*. Workman Publishing Company: New York, NY.

Ortiz, A. (2002). Prevention of school failure and early intervention for English language learners. In A.J. Artiles & A.A. Ortiz (Eds.), *English language learners with special education needs* (pp. 31-48). Washington, D.C.: Center for Applied Linguistics and Delta Publishing.

Ortiz, A. (2006). Parents, families, and special education. *Cultural and linguistic diversity* lecture powerpoint. Austin, TX: University of Texas.

Rayner, K., Foorman, B., Perfetti, C., Pesetsky, D., & Seidenberg, M. (2001, Nov). How psychological science informs the teaching of reading. *Psychological Science in the Public Interest, 2*(2), 31-74.

Richards, R. (1999). *The source for dyslexia and dysgraphia.* Austin, TX: PRO-ED, Inc.

Scott, T., Nelson, C., & Liaupsin, C. (2001, August). Effective instruction: The forgotten component in preventing school violence. *Education and Treatment of Children 24*(3), 309-322.

Shaywitz, S. (2003). *Overcoming dyslexia: A new and complete science-based program for reading problems at any level.* New York, NY: Alfred A. Knopf.

Sutherland, K. & Wehby, J. (2001, March/April). Exploring the relationship between increased opportunities to respond to academic requests and the academic and behavioral outcomes of students with EBD: A review. *Remedial and Special Education 22*(2), 113-121.

Swindoll, C. (1981, 1982). *Attitudes.* Insight for Living: Frisco, TX.

Tolle, E. (1999). *The power of now: A guide to spiritual enlightenment.* Novato, CA: New World Library.

Tribby, M. (2012). *The success indicator info-graphic.* MaryEllen Tribby is the founder of WorkingMomsOnly.com and creator of "*The Success Indicator*" info-graphic 2012.

University of Texas Counseling and Mental Health Center. (2015). Self-esteem. Austin, TX: The University of Texas at Austin. Retrieved January 5, 2018 from https://cmhc.utexas.edu/selfesteem.html.

U.S. Census Bureau. (2012). Table pinc-03: Educational attainment—people 25 years old and over. Retrieved December 9, 2015 from https://www.census.gov/hhes/www/cpstables/032012/perinc/pinc03_000.htm.

Warren, S., Fey, M., & Yoder, P. (2007). Differential treatment intensity, research: A missing link to creating optimally effective communication interventions. *Mental Retardation and Developmental Disabilities Research Reviews 13*, 70-77.

West, T.G. (1997). *In the mind's eye: Visual thinkers, gifted people with dyslexia and other learning difficulties, computer images and the ironies of creativity.* Amherst, NY: Prometheus Books.

Young, S. (2002). *Great failures of the extremely successful: Mistakes, adversity, failure and other steppingstones to success.* Los Angeles, CA: Tallfellow Press.

Made in the USA
San Bernardino, CA
14 August 2019